CRANKY SUPERPOWERS

Life Lessons Learned from the Common CrankaTsuris Chronicles

By Steven Joseph

ENIGAMI IMAGINE
Independent publishing solutions

ENIGAMIIMAGINE
Independent publishing solutions

First published 2023.
This edition published 2023.

The moral rights of the author and artist have been asserted. All rights reserved.

Names: Joseph, Steven, author.

Title: Cranky Superpowers: Life Lessons Learned from the Common CrankaTsuris Chronicles / by Steven Joseph.

Description: First Edition. | Hoboken, New Jersey : Enigami Publishing, 2023.

Summary: New and old stories are given a hysterical laugh-out-loud spin, but ultimately teach us that we all possess "Cranky Superpowers."

Subjects: BISAC: SELF-HELP / Communication & Social Skills | SELF-HELP / Emotions | SELF-HELP / Personal Growth / General | SELF-HELP / Self-Management / General | SELF-HELP / Self-Management / Stress Management | HUMOR / Form / Anecdotes & Quotations

Hardback ISBN: 979-8-9876117-6-0
Paperback ISBN: 979-8-9876117-5-3
e-Book ISBN: 979-8-9876117-4-6
Audio Book ISBN: 979-8-9876117-7-7
LCCN: 2023913847

Snoodle Illustrations by Andy Case
Edited by Deb Lucas
Designed by Jennifer Thomas

CRANKY SUPERPOWERS

Life Lessons Learned from the Common CrankaTsuris Chronicles

By Steven Joseph

ACKNOWLEDGEMENTS

Much thanks and gratitude must be given to my daughter, Vita, who fills my life with joy, my wife, Carolyn, who fills my every day with laughter; to my illustrator, Andy Case, who illustrations are the music to my words; and to Desiree, Dave, and the whole Black Chateau family, who always provide the much-needed encouragement.

And great thanks to Shari Belitz who shared a wonderful memory of her father, Stan Newberger, a person who lived an amazing life that embodied the term "utilizing skillful means." Her words are included in this book.

SPECIAL DEDICATION

This book is especially dedicated to my partner of 20 years, Elena Yuuka Taurke, who passed away on April 18, 2022 after fighting a two-and-a-half-year battle with ALS.

April 18th was the third day of the Jewish holiday of Passover, which celebrates and retells the story of the Exodus from Egypt. While people typically make reference to the "freedom from" bondage, the more important lesson of the holiday is to consider the "freedom to" in our lives. While we may be wandering in the desert, free from being slaves in Egypt, this is not the "freedom to" that we all try to strive towards.

Elena, who grew up with Juvenile Arthritis, spent every day working on her "freedom to." There was freedom to create, freedom to dance, freedom to change, freedom to make us all think, freedom to live, and ultimately even the freedom to die.

There are many odd, and some familiar, characters you will come across in this book. The common thread of all these characters is that they too are about pursuing the freedom to; always going forward and never going backward.

I hope that in reading this book, with a few belly laughs of course, you may find your own "freedom to," just like Elena lived every day of her life.

TABLE OF CONTENTS

PREFACE

This journey of exploring the topic of crankiness began in earnest when I wrote my first book, a children's book titled *The Last Surviving Dinosaur: The TyrantoCrankaTsuris*. This story was about how humans evolved from the smallest most dangerous dinosaur on the planet, the TyrantoCrankaTsuris. The word "tsuris" is the Yiddish word for problems, and while these problems may really be minor everyday inconveniences, they have to be looked at as major events that you would not wish even on your worst enemy.

In my next book titled *A Grownup Guide to Effective Crankiness: The CrankaTsuris Method,* I coined the phrase "the Common CrankaTsuris." I reasoned then that we refer to the cold as the "common cold" despite the fact that we may only have a couple colds in a year.

The Common CrankaTsuris is something you can experience three or four times in the morning alone. Because of that, we have to be more accepting of ourselves and others when a CrankaTsuris may arise. We may need to be a CrankaTsuris doctor. We each may have our own CrankaTsuris Kryptonite, despite any superpowers we may possess.

This exploration into our crankiness actually began when my partner Elena brought me to the Village Zendo, and introduced me to Buddhism. In Buddhism, they teach about the truth of suffering, the truth of the cause of suffering, the truth to the end of suffering, and the truth of the path that leads us to the end of suffering. In Buddhism, desire and ignorance lies at the root of our suffering.

I had lots of fun writing my first book on "Effective Crankiness" and this book, which points to our "Cranky Superpowers." Just imagine what problems I would encounter if I tried to write about "effective suffering." People would take one look at the title and think to themselves, *I already know how to effectively suffer. I married him (or her). I don't need to buy a book about that.*

But we do need to know how to be effectively cranky. We need those Cranky Superpowers. Because it means that all those things that get to us are somehow heard and understood. We get empathy in return. We feel empowered and hopeful where we used to feel hopeless and depressed. Nobody is bad because they are cranky. Also, we get to laugh at ourselves and each other.

Have fun, enjoy some old characters you may recognize, and welcome some new characters as your new friends. Along the way, I hope this book takes you on a path of discovering your own Cranky Superpowers!

CRANKY SUPERPOWERS

Life Lessons Learned from the
Common CrankaTsuris Chronicles

CHAPTER 1

GETTING ON MY NERVES
CRANKATSURIS

SINCE THE BEGINNING OF TIME, everybody has gotten on everybody else's nerves. Nobody is immune from this form of CrankaTsuris. It does not matter if you are a person with a lot of nerve, have some nerve, or have no nerve whatsoever. No matter what category you personally fit in, sure enough, you will get on somebody's nerve, and somebody will be getting on your nerves as well. No nerves are required.

When someone gets on your nerves, and invariably let out a Cranka Tsuris, you immediately have to let the other person know how much nerve that person happens to have.

"Let me tell you. You have a lot of nerve to say such a thing!"

"You know, you have some nerve showing up late like this!"

"Do you know what your problem is? You don't have any nerve!"

It is even possible to have no nerve and have a lot of nerve at the same time and then be told that you have no nerve and a lot of nerve, which gets on a close family member's nerves, and this family member then proceeds to get on your nerves.

The Yiddish word for nerve is "Chutzpah," and it is here that we see this play out, and which every Jewish kid gets to experience at some point growing up.

Mother: You know what your problem is? You do not have any Chutzpah. You need to have some Chutzpah. How else are you going to get anywhere in this world if you do not have any Chutzpah? You see, your father has Chutzpah. Your brother has Chutzpah. Even your baby sister has more Chutzpah than you.

Son: Mom! Do I have to hear your Chutzpah speech again? Really? For once, can you just get off my freakin' back! Enough with the Chutzpah!

Mother: Now, watch your mouth! Don't be so Chutzpadic (meaning "filled with Chutzpah") with me!

The time I first learned about having "a lot of nerve" (and a tremendous amount of Chutzpah) was in Fourth Grade. I went to a Jewish School in the South Bronx. The name of the school was Yeshiva Torah Ve'Emunah. This was a school that poor Jewish parents in the Bronx sent their kids to. The rich families all sent their kids to the Riverdale Academy. My family could never afford that.

The school was named Yeshiva Torah Ve'Emunah, and it was run by Ultra-Orthodox rabbis from Williamsburg, Brooklyn. I always imagined that the best teachers, who lived in Williamsburg, were able to teach in the many Jewish schools in that were actually in Williamsburg. All the less talented teachers in Williamsburg were required to schlep to a school an hour and a half away by train in the Bronx.

Getting back to Fourth Grade, my teacher was Rabbi Scholar. That was his name, and did not necessarily mean that he was actually a scholar. Rabbi Scholar was a huge man, who would sit all day in class smoking a cigar, drinking coffee, taking his many medications, and studying the horse race charts. All of this happened while all the kids would read quietly from the Bible.

One day, a student in the class, Manny Cerezo, who was also known as the Puerto Rican Jew, because of the simple fact that he was the only Puerto Rican Jew in the school, walked in late, holding a ham and cheese sandwich in his hand.

For those people who may not know, ham is never kosher, and it is also even less kosher, if that is possible, to mix meat and dairy.

Now, if it was bad enough to walk late into class in a Religious Jewish school with a ham and cheese sandwich, Manny made matters much worse by asking Rabbi Scholar the following question:

"Hey, Rabb…Do you want a bite of my ham and cheese sandwich?"

Rabbi Scholar's face turned beet red. He proceeded to grab Manny by the shirt collar and stuffed poor Manny underneath his desk. Rabbi Scholar proceeded to kick Manny for the rest of the morning. Since Rabbi Scholar smoked cigars in class, he used Manny as his ashtray. I sat in the first row, and I heard Manny whimpering for the rest of the morning.

Manny had a lot of nerve that morning, and obviously got on Rabbi Scholar's nerves.

Manny never ate a ham and cheese sandwich ever again.

I learned about having "some nerve" in high school. I went to the Bronx High School of Science, and in my senior year, I was in the Drama Class which also meant that I got to be in the school play.

That year, the school play was a musical called *Dark of the Moon*. We all played hillbillies, and there was a drinking scene that the lead members of the cast sang the following chorus:

We are swillin', always swillin' all day and all night long...

We are swillin', always swillin' that smokey mountain corn!

For the first few performances, we pretended to drink this supposedly alcoholic brew. Of course, there was no alcohol in the bottles, but to make it look like "smokey mountain corn," our bottles were all filled with apple juice. However, for the Sunday matinee, somebody who will remain nameless (but, not me!), thought that it would be a fun idea to mix the apple juice with actual alcohol. One cast member put some vodka in each of our bottles. Nobody would ever find out because we would all just drink the brew from the bottle.

Unfortunately, one cast member who will remain nameless (it was not me!), did not want to drink alcohol on stage, and when it was his turn to drink, he spritzed out of his mouth the apple juice and vodka onto the first row.

More unfortunately, it was our drama teacher who got the alcoholic shower while sitting in the first row. His face turned beet red.

The next day, we were all summoned to the principal's office. We were told:

"You kids have some nerve doing a stunt like that on stage!"

The next day, the other cast members and I were given bottles of turpentine and our punishment was that we had to clean all the graffiti off of the school building for the rest of the school year during recess.

We became known as the "anti-graffiti team" and I was appointed team captain. The only problem was that everybody in the school knew about the alcohol episode, and kids started calling me "Turpentine."

Some kids would shout at me while I was scrubbing the graffiti off of the school walls:

"Hey, Turpentine! Do you need a shot glass for your turpentine? You are looking thirsty!"

It turns out that teenagers happen to have a lot of nerve. I tried really hard not to let these taunts get to my nerves. I do have to admit, though. There were many days I came close to pouring a bottle of turpentine over the Shot Glass Kid.

We learned that "having some nerve" has its consequences. We also learned that having some nerve definitely got on too many people's nerves.

In my professional life as a lawyer, the people who get on my nerves the most are those people who do not have any nerves. Unable to make any decision they're always asking which way to go, and what to do. "Should I go left, or should I go right? If I put one foot in front of the other, should I put the left foot or the right foot first, or do I put the right foot in front of the left?"

These people who happen to have no nerve and are therefore unable to make any decision, even to go to the bathroom, also happen to be very nervous all the time. They walk around spreading their nervous energy, which ends up getting on my nerves.

What makes it even worse is the fact that these people with no nerves whatsoever happen to be lawyers. This fact always puzzles me. You see, I studied at the University of Pittsburgh Law School. We were all taught during the first year how to get on people's nerves. We were all taught during the second year how to rub people the wrong way. For the third and final year of law school, we were all taught how to get under people's skin.

These lawyers are expected to be professionals at getting on people's nerves, rubbing them the wrong way, and getting under people's skin. However, the only time when they utilize this skill is when they send out the legal bill for their professional services. These are the same professional services that clearly did not exhibit the fact that they had any nerve whatsoever other than when they got to act very, very nervous.

I also have this observation. When somebody gets on our nerves, we never inform the other person that they are actually on our nerves. Rather, we only inform this person that they are merely *getting* on our nerves, as if to say that they have not quite landed yet.

However, they have landed.

Mission Control: This annoying person has landed!

Annoyed Person: One small step on man's brain. One giant step on mankind's brain.

Oy. I am getting such a headache!

We only express to other people that a person got on our nerves after we took some drastic action.

"Why did you dump the guy?"

"He got on my nerves."

In the late '70s in the Bronx, the most notorious criminal family was known as the Bronx Bombers. They were a tough and ruthless gang, and they were led by Big Boss Billy. Big Boss Billy became the big boss because he knew how to get on people's nerves. He knew how to rub people the wrong way. He knew how to get under people's skin. Because of this, nobody crossed Big Boss Billy.

Big Boss Billy's top enforcer was Fatty Patty, who got the nickname "Fatty Patty Melt." One day, Fatty Patty Melt came to Big Boss Billy, and he told him that he no longer had the nerves to be the top enforcer.

Fatty Patty Melt told Big Boss Billy:

"My nerves are completely shot!"

This apparently got on Big Boss Billy's nerves, and one day, Fatty Patty Melt was nowhere to be seen.

After a couple of weeks, Little Johnny came into Big Boss Billy's office and asked about Fatty Patty Melt.

Little Johnny: So, what happened to Fatty Patty Melt?

Big Boss Billy: He told me that his nerves were completely shot! My top enforcer. That got on my nerves. If I kept him on, it would start to rub me the wrong way, and after that, if I did nuttin, it would start to get under my skin.

Little Johnny: You definitely do not want Fatty Patty Melt under your skin, Billy. So what happened to Fatty Patty Melt?

Big Boss Billy: Let me just say this. May Fatty Patty melt in pieces, if you get the drift.

Little Johnny: Yeah. May Fatty Patty melt in peace.

As all these stories tell you, no matter the amount of nerves or the lack thereof, we get on each other's nerves. There is no way out. It leads to a "Get on My Nerves CrankaTsuris." This condition can be dangerous for the person suffering from this condition or the person who is on the receiving end of this CrankaTsuris. Because of this, it needs to be dealt with as well. Otherwise, you find yourself telling your own story of Poor Fatty Patty Melt.

This does not mean that there is a sure-fire way of ending the Getting on My Nerves CrankaTsuris. There is no known cure. However, there is good news. Since we all get on each other's nerves, we need to acknowledge this fact. If someone gets on your nerves, you cannot react as if you are a virgin when it comes to getting on other people's nerves. Face it. You are just as annoying as everyone else.

With this acknowledgement, it starts to soften up when other people get on your nerves. You can even make a bit light. When do you get on people's nerves? When do you rub people the wrong way? When do you get under someone's skin?

Write this list with your partner. Have your partner make his or her own list. Compare the lists. "I get on your nerves when..." This is not the "You get on my nerves" list. However, this list is about acknowledgement. Maybe, there are a couple of things you can take off. Maybe, there are some things that the two annoying people can agree to leave on.

When you do this, have a glass of wine, and remember, this is being done all in good fun. And most importantly, remember to laugh at yourself a bit here.

As Oscar Wilde once said, "Life is too important to be taken seriously."

And perhaps, that is the cure for Getting on My Nerves CrankaTsuris.

CHAPTER 2

GENIUS BRAIN CRANKATSURIS

OUT OF ALL THE DIFFERENT SPECIALTIES that exist in the medical profession, the most brilliant one of them all is the podiatrist, otherwise known as the foot doctor. I know this because I went to see the foot doctor, and he told me that I had "athlete's foot." Actually, I had athletes' feet, because it turned out that my feet were both very athletic.

The foot doctor gave me instructions on how to treat the athlete's foot, and I went home satisfied, and even felt pretty good that I had athletes foot. It even sounds like something you want to go home and brag about.

Husband: Honey, great news! I have athlete's foot!!

Wife: Wonderful. Just let me know when you get athlete's body.

Think of how we would all look at illness and disease if we just gave them better names, or at least got a bit more creative. Here's an easy example of "not exactly the best name for a condition":

Patient: I am feeling sad and depressed lately.

Doctor: Interesting. I believe that you are suffering from depression.

I am by no means a doctor. However, how does the diagnosis of depression make a depressed person feel any better about their depression? Answer that question for me. Why would you give a depressing diagnosis to a depressed person?

Now, a brain tumor is a very serious condition, and it should be treated very seriously by the best brain surgeon you can find. Yet, imagine how much more enjoyable the conversation would be if you changed the diagnosis of "brain tumor" to "Genius Brain."

Brain Surgeon: I am sorry to tell you, but the x-rays came back positive. It confirmed what I had feared. You have Genius Brain.

Patient: Genius Brain? Oh no. Will I need a brain operation?

Brain Surgeon: The good news is that the genius in your brain appears to be inoperable. We have to monitor this very closely. If your genius becomes operable, we will have to operate, and remove the genius from your brain.

Patient: Well, thank goodness that my genius is inoperable. I have a question. Suppose that it becomes operable, and you remove the genius from my brain. Can the genius grow back?

Brain Surgeon: Yes. That will be a concern. We will always have to do regular brain scans to determine if you ever have any genius growth inside your brain. A genius inside your brain can be very dangerous, and sometimes even fatal.

Patient: Thank you, Doctor.

Brain Surgeon: By the way, how's your athlete's foot coming along?

Patient: Great! I have it on both of my feet, and I rub my hands on them every day. I am hoping to get athlete's hands!

Brain Surgeon: I shouldn't say this because it is not my specialty, but if you went on a diet, and did a bit of exercise, I hear that you may get athlete's body.

Patient: You must have been talking to my wife. She says the same thing.

Now, I always remember George Carlin arguing in one of his stand-up HBO specials: "People think that if you change the name of the condition, you can change the condition. It doesn't happen, cousin. It just doesn't happen."

He is absolutely right. If you rename a brain tumor, and call it "Genius Brain," it is still a serious condition. It certainly would not change the condition. I have given a new name for our "crankiness." It is called the "CrankaTsuris," or how I like to refer to it as the "Common CrankaTsuris."

The name is not meant to change the condition, or even get rid of the condition. The name "CrankaTsuris" is given to our crankiness to allow us to embrace our own crankiness. If we embrace what we wanted to get rid of or feel ashamed of beforehand, it changes our perception.

While it does not eliminate the condition, it softens the condition. It gives it a form, and by giving it both a form, and a fun name, we can then decide exactly how we want to deposit the CrankaTsuris.

Here is a good way of thinking about this. Imagine if you get punched in the face, and you did not see the punch coming. It came out of nowhere. Then, imagine the punch in the face, and you see it coming. You are prepared. You may still get hit in the face, but you can deflect some of the punch. Even if you could not deflect the punch, it will not hurt as much as the punch that you did not see.

Here is another example. Imagine that you are visiting someone's home. You see that they have a nice rug, and the floors have been cleaned. You ask politely if you should take off your shoes, or the host may even tell you to remove your shoes. You can still walk on the rug, but you are not bringing in the dirt from outside that was on the bottom of your shoes.

Again, by changing the name of the condition, we do not change the condition. However, by changing the name of our crankiness, it reminds us that we always have a choice to be ineffective with our own crankiness or use it effectively. This is what the CrankaTsuris Method is all about.

CHAPTER 3

TEACHING THE OLD DOG NEW TRICKS CRANKATSURIS

IT IS THE START OF A NEW YEAR. Thank goodness. As with any new year, we begin with our New Year's resolutions. However, I have discovered that while many people are quick to come up with their own New Year's resolutions, when it comes time to hear their loved ones state their resolution, the loved one who is informed of this resolution has this negative attitude that dampens the whole New Year's resolution thing.

They ruin it for everyone with one negative comment:

"You can't teach an old dog new tricks."

Because of this, I have decided to bring a class action defamation lawsuit on behalf of all the old dogs. This is an outrage. These comments are being made recklessly without any foundation. How many tricks did these teachers try to teach the old dogs? Was the teacher even a certified new trick teacher? Who is exactly the one who keeps the records of failed attempts of learning new tricks? What even constitutes a "new trick"? Perhaps, it was an old trick that someone thought of saying it was a new trick? Did all of the teachers of the "new tricks" happen to be "young dogs"? I hear that the young dogs have little experience at teaching. They know few of the old tricks, and they are not much good with the new tricks either.

In fact, when a young dog learns a new trick, guess who happens to be the teacher? It is the old dog. In other words, if it is the old dog teaching the young dog the new tricks, the only plausible conclusion is that the old dog was taught the new tricks by another old dog. If an old dog taught the new tricks, the only plausible conclusion we can come to is that an old dog, in fact, can learn the new tricks.

In fact, the real problem, I hear, is that you can't teach a young dog an old trick. They are only a few months old, and they think they are ready to take over the world. They do not care about the old tricks. These young dogs only want to learn the new tricks. They do not realize that you cannot go straight to the new tricks until you learn the old tricks. The "old school" dogs knew that you had to first learn how to play fetch with a ball before you move up to a frisbee. If I had to pick my ultimate frisbee team, I would pick the old dogs every time.

Seriously, the saying about the "old dog" and the "new tricks" has to do with stubbornness. This is more about the person who does not believe in a New Year's resolution. This person is more interested in keeping everything the same, even if it does not work. This stubborn person has the false belief that the more things stay the same, the more they can hold to this misconceived notion of power.

However, what happens if we propose to the stubborn person, who doesn't want to change, that their New Year's resolution should be to obtain more power? Of course, this person was quite powerful the year before. However, this year, the person who we call the "stubborn one" will be even more powerful than that.

The Stubborn One hears this with great interest. "More power for me? I love it! Tell me how! Sign me up!"

Typically, the stubborn one is also the cranky one. The stubborn one is not only cranky but is typically ineffectively cranky. Ineffective crankiness means that nobody really hears you, and you become a bit crankier. You get more consumed with getting your way. You have no time to listen to everyone else. Because you are frustrated by your own stubbornness, you just walk out in frustration, and the only thing on your mind is to figure out how to get your way.

When I titled my last book *A Grownup Guide to Effective Crankiness,* the one implication was that you need to be a grownup. The first step to Effective Crankiness in this new year is to accept the responsibility of a grownup. Think of the small child and define some negative qualities of the stubborn cranky child, and then, turn it over and just write down how a grownup would act. The child may not pay attention. The grownup does. The child may grab and demand things. The grownup may ask politely and say thank you. The child is solely focused on his or her self. The grownup is concerned for others. The child has temper tantrums. The grownup knows how to stay calm when the situation calls for the grownup to be calm.

This is about taking power. This could be the year that we are just the fallen leaf blowing in the wind. Or it may be the year that we are the tree that is firmly planted in the ground. The tree is the one who wields all the power.

The best thing about this New Year's resolution is that it is not about teaching an old dog any new tricks. In fact, the only tricks that an old dog has to learn and re-learn are those tricks much older than the dog.

CHAPTER 4

CRANKATSURIS TIME-OUT

RIGHT AFTER MY DAUGHTER HAD BEEN BORN, I was given a number of instruction manuals on how my child works, and how I can get my child to work better. Of course, each instruction manual had completely different instructions for the proper use of the child. However, it seemed like all the instruction manuals had one idea in common: The Time-Out.

The instruction manuals advised the parents that when a child misbehaves or gets a bit out of control, perhaps with a CrankaTsuris, it is important to put the child in a time-out. The time-out place is typically the child's room. So, in other words, the time-out turned out to be a fancy term for parents to use when they say to the child, "Go up to your room!"

This concept of a "time-out" was rather foreign to me. I do recall that there was one time when I misbehaved as a child, and I was sent to sit on my knees in a corner, staring at a wall with my hand clasped behind me, as if they were tied with an invisible rope. I had to sit there quietly for half an hour.

There was also some requirement, I recall, to be in some state of terror when you were placed into the corner. This was in order that you could feel like you had been kidnapped or taken hostage and that if you made any improper move, your short life might come to a horrible ending. In fact, when this occurred, I actually had the thought race through my head that the two people in the other room were not actually my parents. Rather, they were just pretending to be my parents until the time when my real parents paid the ransom.

But, the real reason that the concept of a "time-out" was so foreign to me was because I did not really grow up with many time-outs. I had to endure something much worse. I had to go through about eighteen years of a "time-in." If you are trying to teach discipline to your child, a "time-in" gets the message across way better than any time-out could.

Both my father and my mother had their own "time-ins." My father's mantra to both my brother and to me was to leave our bedroom and "come and sit with the family." Since it was just my brother, me, and my parents, sitting with the family just meant sitting with my parents.

My father had a rule for sitting at the table during mealtimes. Nobody was allowed to leave the table until my father was finished eating. If we were done, we had to sit quietly, and with no elbows on the table. This all happened while my father would eat with his mouth wide open and the television blasting in the background.

Once my father was had finished eating, my father would order us: "Come sit with the family." My father went from the dining room to the living room, and the television was now turned on there at full blast. My father was lying on the recliner chair, and my mother was on the couch. I would have to sit on the carpet near the television.

The reason for my particular position was that this was a time before the remote control was invented. Because I was the youngest in the family, I had to be the remote control.

Sunday mornings were particularly tough for an eight-year-old kid. My father would watch exciting shows like "Meet the Press," "Face the Nation," and the "McLaughlin Report" all at the same time. Depending on the guest of each show, I had to get up and switch from channel to channel to channel. I was introduced to remote control aerobics at an early age.

I went years fantasizing that, one day, I would grow up and invent a remote control so that kids like me would not be put into forced remote control labor. To my disappointment, some other kid that came before me had the exact same fantasy because, by the 1980s, somebody actually invented the remote control, and it was available with every television.

Unfortunately, at the same time that the remote control became available in every household, cable TV also came on to the scene. Instead of going between six different channels, there were now over a hundred channels to choose from. My father, who apparently was the first person to come down with Attention Deficit Disorder, was given full control of the remote.

I was out of a job, but I had to lie on the floor in front of the television, and my father, with the remote in hand, had changing channels down to a science. At the very minute that I started getting into the story of a particular show, my father changed the channel. Also, in the old days, you would change the channel from channel 4 to channel 7, and that was it. Now, changing the channel was to go from channel 1 to 2 to 3 to 4,897. Ok. We did not have 4,897 channels but it certainly felt that way.

The one thing that actually saved me from this channel change torture was that my father always seemed to fall asleep by the time he got to channel 3000. Channel 3000 never had any good shows on, and it was always in some language that I did not understand. But with the remote still tightly in my father's grip, I never took the chance of trying to pull it out of his hand. I would rather watch a Spanish soap opera, not knowing what anyone was saying, than sit once again through the remote control changing torture!

My mother had a completely different method to the "time-in." Actually, my mother invented the original "time-out," which was her own "time-in." I look back at this time with great affectionate feelings of nostalgia.

My mother never asked me to do anything for her. Not a single favor. At least, it was not in the normal way a person might ask another person to do a favor. There was no "do this" or "do that." Instead, she would make requests with the beginning of "the ask" to be "Steveee, do you feel like…"

These requests were not made with the notion of curiosity of how I actually did feel about going on a trip to the beauty parlor. The only answer that was allowed would be:

"Yes!! That is exactly what I feel like doing! By the way, my friends had asked me if I was interested in going to the beach since it is the fifteenth day straight of this heatwave that we are all suffering through. Of course, who would feel like going to the beach with friends, and taking a dip into the ocean when you have the opportunity to go to the beauty parlor! Thank you! I will be ready to go in a minute."

Now, I said "Going to." I did not say "Take me." I was still young and did not have a car. My mother did not drive, and the beauty parlor was not around the corner. We would have to wait for the BX17 bus (that did not have air conditioning, by the way) to go from Co-op City in the Bronx to Allerton Avenue in the Pelham Parkway neighborhood nearby. That took an hour. Then, my mother had to wait till a hairdresser was available. Another half an hour. Finally, they would call her, and do the wash, cut, and curl. The curl was to put my mother's hair in curlers. An hour and a half. Once that was done, my mother was seated next to all the other ladies in curlers, and they would sit with the space hat dryer things over their heads. That took an hour and seemed like another three hours. I just sat and sat and sat. Finally, when my mother was done, we went out and had to wait for the BX17 bus again, without air conditioning, to come to go back home.

Once we got on the bus six hours later, my mother would calmly ask me:

"Stevee, do you feel like going to the butcher with me?"

Because I grew up suffering through time-ins, time-outs seemed rather weird to me. You mean to tell me that if I want to go up to my room, all I have to do is a bit of misbehaving? Really? That is so cool. I will make sure that I will misbehave at least three or four times a day! This is an excellent deal. I will make sure to give a nice present around holiday time to whoever the negotiator was that you hired to come up with this great deal for me!

You may have noticed that I am not a firm believer in either the "time-in" or the "time-out" but I am a firm believer in Effective Crankiness or the CrankaTsuris Method, I do believe it is not a bad idea to have a bit of quiet time. However, it is important to understand the particular CrankaTsuris that led to quiet time and using the CrankaTsuris once the quiet time has ended.

I want to use the example of two brothers, Jimmy and Timmy. Jimmy takes Timmy's toy. Timmy starts to cry. The boys start to fight. Jimmy, the culprit, is sent to his room. Timmy, who got upset, is also sent to a quiet place to calm down as well.

When Jimmy and Timmy return, and everybody is a bit calmer, we explain the rules. It is okay to be cranky and it is okay to want something. But, when you take something that is not yours, someone else gets cranky (has a CrankaTsuris) and because it happens to be his toy, he may actually want the toy as well.

Now, I am a big fan of Dr. Seuss. There are the cute rhymes, and it is filled with silliness. Using the CrankaTsuris, but in a fun way, we can now create our own Dr. Seuss story.

There is one character who takes another character's toy and does a CrankaTsuris.

"I take the toy on a boat. I take the toy with a goat. I take the toy on a float. I take the toy in a coat. I take the toy on a train. I take the toy on a plane. I take the toy in the rain."

The response then can be:

"You take the toy on a boat? You take the toy with a goat? You take the toy on a float? You take the toy in a coat? You take the toy on a train? You take the toy on a plane? You take the toy in the rain? … You are making us insane!"

The original CrankaTsuris that caused Jimmy and Timmy to go up to their rooms typically has created one or both of the parental authorities to have a headache, perhaps one that is on top of a headache they already had. I give the term headache a new name. I call it "heggetz." They are giving me a bad heggetz! Oy!!

"You are giving me a heggetz. My head is full of meggetz. They are crawling with their leggetz. I am feeling both schweggetz and schlegetz. The heggetz is even causing some pleggetz. It is not because I ate too many eggetz, but I will need to see some meddeccs!"

There are endless variations to this. In my book *The Last Surviving Dinosaur*, there were three dinosaurs who made fun of the small TyrantoCrankaTsuris until the TyrantoCrankaTsuris let out the biggest most ferocious CrankaTsuris the world had ever heard. We are teaching "cause and effect" but in a fun way, replacing the badness associated with crankiness with a bit of understanding and a whole lot of empathy.

Of course, if this does not work, you can always try out the "time-in." Good luck!

"So we learned to express our inner TyrantoCrankaTsuris or TyrantoKvetchaTsuris too often. Just the right amount to keep the planet happy and not too cranky."

Taken from my book *The Last Surviving Dinosaur: The Tyranto-CrankaTsuris.*

CHAPTER 5

CINDERELLA CRANKATSURIS

ONCE UPON A TIME, in a land far, far away, there lived a little girl named Ella. Ella had a childhood everyone wished they could have. She had two warm and loving parents, Brucie and Frannie Wayne, and they lived in a big mansion overseeing the largest city in the kingdom. The city was called Gothingham.

Bruce and Frannie Wayne made their fortune in the shoe business. There was nobody else that could match the beautiful shoes that they were able to produce at their shoe factory that was called "The Wayne Shoe Foundation." The most precious of the different model shoes that they made were their special ruby red slippers. The ruby red slippers were the most coveted shoes in the entire kingdom, and many believed that the slippers contained special powers that would protect anyone wearing the shoes from any kind of evil or harm.

On the other side of the kingdom lived the Wicked Witch. She spent her day doing all sorts of fun and wicked things. But even with her wickedness, she was not able to get her own pair of ruby red slippers. The problem with the slippers was that if you were already living an evil life, you could not wear the slippers because that would protect yourself from yourself.

One day, the Wicked Witch concocted a plan to wait outside the ballet theater that Bruce and Frannie always took their daughter Ella, to on Sundays. Ella was quite fond of the ballet, and she loved going to the ballet with her parents wearing her ruby red slippers.

The Wicked Witch had just used a spell to turn Prince Frankie into a frog. It had worked so well that the Wicked Witch decided she was going to use this spell to turn the entire Wayne family into frogs. She believed that if she turned Ella into a frog she could then do another spell to turn herself to look like Ella. If the Wicked Witch looked like Ella, she could then wear the ruby red slippers. Once she had the ruby red slippers on her feet, she could then do another spell to change back into her old Wicked Witch self.

That Sunday, just as the Wayne family were leaving the theater, the Wicked Witch approached them. Quickly, she cast a spell on Brucie and Frannie, and they turned into frogs. But, because Ella was wearing the ruby red slippers protecting her from both evil and harm, the spell cast on Ella backfired, and the Wicked Witch herself transformed into a fly.

Now that Brucie and Frannie were frogs, they quickly developed frog habits, and started to chase down the fly. They were able to catch the fly, who just moments earlier, had been a wicked witch, and together they shared the fly as their first frog meal.

Ella was left all alone. She completely lost all memory of her past, even her name. Mysteriously, the ruby red slippers disappeared from her feet.

Frannie's sister was a woman who lived alone with her three daughters. Her name was Maize Rapunzel, and her daughters were named Raize, Staize, and Traize. Momma Maizie, as the closest relative, took in Ella as her stepchild. However, she was not kind at all. She did not tell Ella the real story about her parents. She simply told Ella that her parents had abandoned her. Momma Maize immediately put Ella to work, cleaning the house all day, and preparing meals. Also, because all of the Rapunzels had very long hair, the sinks and bathtubs in the house would always get clogged up, and it was Ella's job every day to unclog the sinks and the bathtub.

Momma Maize made Ella sleep in the basement where it was very dusty and dirty. Also, because the Rapunzels wanted the bathtub clear for themselves, it was only on a rare occasion that Ella was allowed to take a bath. Because Ella was always filthy from the cinder dust, the Rapunzels all called Ella "Cinderella."

Momma Maize took over the Wayne's shoe factory, and renamed all of the shoe stores that the Wayne family had previously run to The Marvelous Mrs. Maize's Shoe Emporium. However, nobody thought that the shoes were all that marvelous. No matter what Momma Maize tried, she could not duplicate the ruby red slippers that the Waynes had manufactured.

This got Momma Maize even madder than she had been before. One day, she decided that Cinderella brought her bad luck, and that was the reason that Momma Maize could not duplicate the magical ruby red slippers. Momma Maize concocted a plan to bring home a poisonous snake and put the snake in the basement room that Cinderella slept in. The snake would poison Cinderella, and once Cinderella was gone, Momma Maize would then be able to make the magical ruby red slippers. Everyone in the kingdom would then proclaim her as "The Marvelous Mrs. Maize"!

That night, after Cinderella was fast asleep, Momma Maize snuck down into the room, and let the snake out that she had carried in her basket. The snake immediately slithered over to Cinderella. Just as the snake was about to take a bite out of her, Cinderella woke up startled and started speaking to the snake. The snake was excited that he was able to understand every word that Cinderella had said. They talked with each other all night long, and quickly became friends.

Cinderella was very excited to have a new best friend. She was even more excited that the snake was able to fit in the drains of all the sinks and the bathtub, helping Cinderella unclog them. When Momma Maize would check up on Cinderella and the snake, the snake always hid away. Momma Maize decided not to plot any further against Cinderella because she thought that Cinderella became quite good at unclogging drains. Momma Maize reasoned that Cinderella was needed because, as we know, all of the Rapunzels had such long hair which, of course, clogged all of the drains on a daily basis.

The three sisters, Raize, Staize, and Traize were lazy and crazy, and also very mean to Cinderella. They would boss Cinderella around all day, especially instructing her to put away all the shoes that Momma Maize would bring home for them.

The sisters also spent most of the day either washing, combing or blow drying their hair. At least five or six times a day, the sisters would approach Cinderella and ask her if she thought that their hair was beautiful.

Raize would say: "Our hair is so shiny."

Staize would say: "Our hair is so silky."

Traize would say: "Our hair is so long."

Cinderella would always just respond politely by saying that yes, of course, their hair was not only beautiful, but was also so shiny, so silky and so long. Because Cinderella was not able to bathe much, her hair was not so beautiful, or so shiny, silky or long. Cinderella never complained, and always did whatever tasks her three mean stepsisters demanded that she do.

On the other side of town, not far from the mansion where the Wayne family estate stood, was the Royal Palace. This is where the King, Queen, and Prince Frankie lived. As we have said, years earlier, the Wicked Witch used a spell to turn Prince Frankie into a frog. A year earlier, Prince Frankie—known back then as "Frankie the Frog"—saw a delicious fly land on a young lady named Snow White.

Snow White herself had been put into a deep sleep when the Wicked Witch tricked Snow White into eating a poisonous apple.

Snow White would only be able to wake up if a prince approached her and kissed her lips. Frankie the Frog was so grateful for the delicious fly meal that he found on Snow White's face, he gave Snow White a big thankful kiss. Immediately, Snow White woke up and Prince Frankie turned back into human form.

Everyone in the kingdom, including Snow White, assumed that Prince Frankie and Snow White would get married and live happily ever after. However, after nine months of dating, Prince Frankie broke up with Snow White. After the breakup, Prince Frankie paced every day throughout the castle. It became obvious to everyone that Prince Frankie was feeling very cranky. The King and Queen, upset that Prince Frankie broke up with Snow White, summoned Prince Frankie into their private chambers.

King: You seem upset. Why don't you just get back together with Snow White?

Queen: My dear Frankie, she seems like such a nice girl. Besides, a prince who was once a frog cannot be so picky.

Prince: I told you the story. It just did not work out. First, she insisted on living with seven dwarves. What kind of a girl lives with seven dwarves?

King: You know. When I met your mother, she was living with four giants.

Prince: That was different. The four giants were guarding the castle. Snow White is always busy cooking and cleaning after these seven dwarves. I witnessed this. They may have been very little, but they were all huge slobs. With the mess they made, it was getting crazy. It was like living with seven little children!

Queen: You have to understand. This is destiny. You had the magical kiss with Snow White. Everyone in the kingdom wants to see you two get married.

Prince: I will tell you again. It was not a kiss. It was a meal. The meal happened to be on Snow White's lips.

King: I do not have to tell you again. When you were a frog, your mother cried herself to sleep every night. "What kind of queen would have a frog for a son," she cried!

Prince: You know. Sometimes, all I want is to be turned back into a frog. It was not so bad being a frog. When I was a frog, this wonderful frog couple Brucie and Frannie Frog took me in and treated me like their own son. One night, they showed me in their frog home a pair of ruby red slippers. They told me that, one day, I will turn back to human form. They explained to me that when I did, I was to take the ruby red slippers and place them on the feet of the person who would one day be my bride. Once the shoes were placed on her feet, she just would have to say "There is no place like home." Something magical is then supposed to happen, and I would know that this girl was the right girl for me.

King: So, did you ever try putting the ruby red slippers on Snow White's feet?

Prince: I did, and Snow White did say "There is no place like home."

Queen: So, that is good. What happened?

Prince: The seven dwarves came over and gave us a group hug. I can tell you. None of the seven dwarves ever learned how to take a bath. They all stunk like a sewer.

Queen: This is not important. Everyone is talking about it. You do know that Snow White came out with her autobiography *Snow White and the Seven Dwarves*. It was such a big hit; you know, it even became a major motion picture. They are playing it in all the movie theaters. I saw the movie the other night. It was great! Do you know how the movie ended?

Prince: This is what makes me crazy. This is why I am pacing up and down the halls every day, brooding. Do you really want to know the reason we broke up? Snow White always got insulted when I referred to the seven dwarves as "dwarves." She would always try to correct me and say "They are not dwarves. They are seven cute little men." Day after day, I had to hear Snow White complaining about that. I always had to hear how insensitive I was. And what does she do once we break up? She puts out a best-selling book called *Snow White and the Seven Dwarves*. I tell you: Snow White is a vengeful person. She cannot be trusted.

King: I understand. But do you have a plan B?

Prince: In fact, I do. I have been chatting online on the computer recently with this girl named Cinderella. She lives with her stepmother and three stepsisters. Apparently, they are very mean to her, and they never let Cinderella out of the house. When the three stepsisters are away, she sneaks on to the computer, and that is how we talk.

Queen: Cinderella. It sounds like such a dirty name. I already do not like her.

King: Even if you chat on the computer, it is still not the same as meeting in person. You have to admit at least, the music in the movie *Snow White and the Seven Dwarves* is fabulous. Your mother ordered the album on Amazon, and she plays the soundtrack to the movie just before we go to bed.

Queen: It's my favorite album. Snow White has such a beautiful voice.

Prince: I have a plan. Okay. I am going to throw a big party at the palace next Saturday night. I will have the servants send out invitations to every maiden in the land. And yes. I will even send out an invitation to Snow White.

King: Wait a second. I like the plan, but this Cinderella. You say she is never allowed to leave the house.

Prince: I know. But we have been talking. Cinderella tells me that she plans to hook up with a fairy godmother that she ordered online, and this fairy godmother will magically transform her into a beautiful princess. She will arrive in a stagecoach meant for a princess. Once she arrives at the palace, I will put the ruby red slippers on her feet. She will then say "There is no place like home." I assure you. Something will happen. You will see.

Queen: Son! You are living in a fairy tale. So, tell me. What happens if nothing happens.

Prince: If nothing happens, you have my word. I will get back together with Snow White, and Snow White and I will get married. I have to warn you that the seven dwarves will have to move into the palace so it may be a bit smelly here.

Queen: No worries. We will make sure they all get bathed.

That Saturday evening, the big palace ball blasts off. Everyone who is anyone is there. However, there is no sign of Cinderella. The three Rapunzel sisters approach the Prince.
"Our hair is so shiny," says Raize.
"Our hair is so silky," says Staize
"Our hair is so long," says Traize.
The Prince, frustrated, thinks to himself that Raize, Staize, and Traize are indeed crazy.
Snow White then approaches the Prince.

Snow White: Did you see the movie? In the ending, we get married and live happily ever after!

Prince: No. I refuse to see that movie. And we are not getting married. I told you. I do not want to spend the rest of my life with seven dwarves.

Snow White: They are not dwarves. They are cute little men.

Prince Frankie walks away disgusted, and mutters to himself "dwarves."

Snow White: I heard that. They are not dwarves. They are cute little men!

Meanwhile, at the Rapunzel home, Cinderella and her snake friend begin to chant following exactly the instructions she saw online to summon the fairy godmother. Sure enough, Cinderella's fairy godmother appears.

Cinderella approached her fairy godmother.

Cinderella: Oh, Fairy Godmother. You are here. Thank goodness! I am ready for you. Transform me into a beautiful princess. Take whatever you need, and turn a pumpkin, a potato, whatever, into a beautiful carriage. There are mice outside and you can turn them into well-dressed horsemen. Hurry. I am late. I have to meet the Prince.

Fairy Godmother: Nope. No ball gown. No carriage. No horsemen.

Cinderella: I don't understand… But, in the book… I read the book online… It was on the internet. That is what I put an order in for!

Fairy Godmother: First of all, you can't believe everything you read on the internet. Second, I did bring you something. I will take it out of my bag. It is a megaphone. Try it out. I put in fresh batteries.

Cinderella grabbed the megaphone and started to scream into it.

Cinderella: A megaphone? You brought me only a megaphone? You gotta be freakin kidding me. You think that I pretended to be nice all these years, being a martyr just to be given a lousy megaphone? Do you think I enjoyed cooking and cleaning up after these Rapunzel witches? Do you think I enjoyed listening to Raize, Staize and Traize everyday say repeatedly over and over again, "Isn't our hair shiny? Isn't our hair silky? Isn't our hair long?" Now, if I do not get a prince tonight, I am going to report you to the Better Fairy Godmother Business Bureau. This is so unacceptable! I will tell you. This is beyond outrageous.

Cinderella was so loud cranking out her tsuris on the megaphone, it was heard above all the noise at the ball. Prince Frankie immediately recognized Cinderella's voice and sent his best horsemen to bring Cinderella to the castle.

Once at the castle, Prince Frankie brought out the ruby red slippers, and placed them on the feet of Cinderella. He asked Cinderella to chant the words "There is no place like home."

Cinderella chanted the words, and two frogs jumped through the window, leap-frogging over to Prince Frankie and Cinderella. Prince Frankie immediately recognized the frogs as Brucie and Frannie.

Prince Frankie then turned to Brucie and Frannie, and asked them what they were doing there.

Brucie and Frannie said together: "Give Cinderella a kiss, and you shall understand."

Prince Frankie gave Cinderella a kiss, and Brucie and Frannie immediately returned to their human form. Cinderella looked at them as if she had just woken up from a dream, and said "Momma! Poppa!" They all wept and gave each other a big hug.

The next day, Prince Frankie and Cinderella got married and they lived happily ever after. Brucie and Frannie reopened their shoe factory and once again, began producing beautiful ruby red slippers.

By the way, a year later, the movie *Cinderella* came out, and it was a big hit. Nobody wanted to see *Snow White and the Seven Dwarves* anymore. Apparently, everyone started to think that it was just not so nice to call those seven cute little men "dwarves."

CHAPTER 6

THE GRAND REOPENING
NEW AND IMPROVED CRANKATSURIS

THERE ARE TWO PHRASES THAT I HAVE UNDERSTOOD, but could never understand why they have been used so much:

"Grand Reopening"

"New and Improved"

I looked up the word "grand" in the dictionary, and a synonym for "grand" is "magnificent." I cannot speak for anyone else, but for me, getting to "magnificent" is a pretty high bar to reach.

Just because a restaurant finally got rid of all the cockroaches in the bathroom, this does not make the reopening of the restaurant magnificent.

Just because the restaurant finally got rid of the mice in the kitchen, this does not make the reopening of the restaurant magnificent.

Just because the toilet finally flushes properly, this does not make the reopening of the restaurant magnificent.

And just because the restaurant finally got the sign "Condemned by the Department of Health" removed, that definitely does not make the reopening of the restaurant magnificent.

I lived in Nyack, New York for many years, and at least once a week I went to the local Chinese take-out place to get Chinese food for dinner. This tiny hole in the wall was in Nyack forever. However, they always had a huge "Grand Reopening" banner in front that you could not miss when walking in.

Finally, one day, I had to ask the owner why he kept the "Grand Reopening" sign up for so many years. Surely, at some point, you should not be able to advertise "Grand Reopening."

The owner pointed to the sign that said "Hours of Operation."

"What time does restaurant close?" he asked me.

"Twelve AM," I replied.

"What time does restaurant open?" he then asked.

"Twelve PM," I answered.

He then said to me, "Twelve PM. This is the Grand Reopening."

I guess he had a point.

The other phrase "New and Improved" is a phrase that I have even more problems with. First, we are all getting "Old and Slowly Decaying" so it only makes sense that when I go to the store to make my purchases, I should just be sent to the "Old and Slowly Decaying" section.

Of course, the bigger problem is that they never really tell you exactly what is new and improved. I bought the "New and Improved" toothpaste and took it home with me. I looked on the box to see what the "Active Ingredient" was. That is another term that gives me trouble, "Active Ingredient." As we all know, the "Active Ingredient" for toothpaste is fluoride. I took a look at my old tube of toothpaste, and read that this is the active ingredient. Of course, when I looked at the "New and Improved" toothpaste, it had the same one "Active Ingredient": Fluoride.

So, if the "New and Improved" toothpaste is "New and Improved" because they have only improved their "Inactive Ingredients," please explain to me how this toothpaste is now "New and Improved." I certainly can understand if they would explain to me, "You know that ingredient that was inactive for so many years? Well, we finally figured out to turn that inactive ingredient into an active one!"

Why should any product have so many inactive ingredients put in there in the first place? I think that some marketing genius should put a big label on their packaging "Made with only Active Ingredients." Those "100% Active Ingredients" products would just fly off the shelf.

ACTIVE INGREDIENT:
Permethrin: [*3-Phenoxyphenyl) methyl
    (±) cis/trans 3-(2,2-dichloroethenyl)-2,2-
    dimethylcyclopropanecarboxylate] 2.5%
OTHER INGREDIENTS 97.5%
                                            Total   100.0%

*cis/trans isomer ratio: Min 35% (±) cis
Max 65% (±) trans

KEEP OUT OF REACH OF CHILDREN
CAUTION See Booklet For Additional
Precautionary Statements

There is only one thing in the entire universe that you can actually use the phrases "Grand Reopening" *and* "New and Improved" about. Although they are not actually a thing, but a musical group; I am talking about the Beatles.

The 1970s consumed my grade school and high school years, and that was the time I was getting into music. The Beatles had already broken up, but I heard about them, and I saved my allowance to first buy the "Red Album" which was their Greatest Hits from 1962 to 1966.

I listened to it constantly. It never left the turntable. I then saved up some more money and bought the "Blue Album" which was the Beatles Greatest Hits from 1967-1970.

It was even better. It really was both a "Grand Reopening" and "New and Improved."

I can mention another band that had a "Reopening," and it was "New." However, I personally cannot say it was both "Grand" and "Improved."

I am talking about the Peter Gabriel Genesis, and the Phil Collins Genesis. Now, the Phil Collins Genesis was way more popular, had many more hits, but I am sorry. Yes. It was a reopening and it was new. Maybe, this just has to do with my own personal taste in music. However, I just cannot say this was both "Grand" and "Improved."

While I do think that both the phrases "Grand Reopening" and "New and Improved" are quite overused, I do believe that these phrases can be perfectly appropriate when we try to think of "Effective Crankiness," and our CrankaTsuris Method.

In *A Grownup Guide to Effective Crankiness,* there is a chapter that is titled "CrankaTsuris Diet." This tells the story of my journey towards losing 85 pounds in five months. I talk about changing our "normals" in that Chapter. We should always try to look for healthy "normals" to replace those "normals" that may have not worked out so well for us.

However, if we want to get to "Grand Reopening" and "New and Improved," we cannot confuse the word "normal" with the word "habit."

"Habit" is a word that is more temporary. You could develop a good habit, and then slowly revert to your old bad habits. It sounds like a diet, and it is why diets rarely work.

A "Normal" is something that is permanent. Think about this conversation that could never really happen:

Worker comes into the office, and is greeted by the Boss.

Boss: Did you forget something today?

Worker: I do not think so. Why do you ask?

Boss: You are completely naked.

Worker: So?

Boss: Tell me if I am wrong, but didn't you always come in to work wearing clothes?

Worker: Yes. Yes. I did wear clothes. I just thought that if I changed my habit of wearing clothes to just going naked, I can get in to work much earlier, and be much more productive.

Boss: That is what I call taking initiative. I will tell you what. I will give you a promotion and a raise. Hey, maybe now, you can even afford some clothes.

If you are looking for a habit, whether good or bad, you are simply looking for a spot to park your car in. It is just temporary. However, if you are choosing a new "normal," you are looking to build your home.

"Normals" are way more permanent. If someone came into work naked, do not be too surprised if there is someone that will tell you that this can be characterized as "abnormal." There may even be somebody to take you off to the Funny Farm.

So, please remember that the word "habit" is not a word that we use in the *Grownup Guide to Effective Crankiness*. It is not part of the CrankaTsuris Method. If we become mindful to adopt our better normals, we can then finally have our "Grand Reopening" and declare that we are both "New" and "Improved."

And you may even be able to turn an "inactive" ingredient into an "active" one!

CHAPTER 7

CRANKATSURIS MENOPAUSE

THE OTHER DAY, I had received a flattering review on my last book, *A Grownup Guide to Effective Crankiness.* This female reviewer wrote:

> "If only the author was female. I'd love a book like this on menopause."

It is true that I am not a woman, and I would not dare to write on the hot flash afflictions women may carry as a result of going through menopause. However, as a CrankaTsuris expert, I do have the solution to CrankaTsuris Menopause. The reason that I can do that is that I just got married. Not only did I just get married to a woman who I love dearly and with whom I have been together for close to ten years, but she happens to be right in the middle of her menopause cycle. I have been with her from the beginning of this situation, and we got married just so I can see this cycle calmly fade away, just like a soft ocean wave retreating back into the ocean.

Before I provide you with my solution to this problem, part of this problem arises from the wedding vows we take. If we examine those vows closely, we can understand the problem, and by understanding the problem, we can then come up with a proper solution.

First, I have to tell you the story of my parents. It is a lovely story. My father immigrated to Israel after World War II, and worked for ZIM Shipping Company. My father essentially worked full time on a ship, but he went to different ports of call, and sure enough, one of those stops was in New York.

My father then somehow arranged to have a blind date with my mother. My father took my mother to the Horn and Hardart Automated Coffee Shop that was located on 42nd Street near the United Nations. He bought my mother a cup of coffee for five cents, and right there on the first date, my father proposed to my mother. My mother, amazingly enough, said "Yes." They then got married in New York, New Jersey, and Connecticut because they believed if they got married in enough states, it would be easier for my father to become an American citizen.

My parents would always explain to me that the reason they did this was because they were "Greenhorns." Growing up, I was convinced that "Greenhorn" was actually my real last name.

Years later, I asked my mother how she could say yes on the first date after just a cup of coffee. My mother smiled at me, almost chuckling, and said in her syrupy sweet voice:

"He looked like a hard worker."

That was the only criteria for my mother, so it was really easy for her. However, the wedding vows we take are way more complicated. We do not even answer the questions right. We are asked if we take this woman or man for better or for worse; in sickness and in health. People think that it is a "Yes" or "No" question, but it is not. It is a choice. Which one? For better or for worse? In sickness or in health? Of course, let's imagine what fun we would have if couples did answer the question the right way giving serious consideration to the choices they are making.

Priest: Seymour, do you take this woman for better or for worse?

Seymour: You know, I would like to say better. But my bride Zelda here gets very nervous. If I say "better," it would put too much pressure on her. Anyway, I am not marrying a beauty queen. So, how much worse can worse be?

Priest: It can get a lot worse. This is what I hear.

Seymour: I'll take a chance. Put me down for "worse."

Priest: Zelda, do you take Seymour for better or for worse?

Zelda: Definitely better. You know how it is. If you are picking from the bottom of the barrel, you can't really get much worse. So, I am going with "better."

Seymour: Look who is talking about "bottom of the barrel"! Priest, I want to change my answer to "better."

Zelda: How does this work exactly? What if I think he is getting me "better," but Seymour thinks I got worse? Or what if the opposite happens? To be honest with you, Seymour here wants me better. I do not know if I can do better.

Seymour: I said better. You have to do better. That is why the priest gives us the option.

Zelda: What a hypocrite you are.

Turning to the priest, Zelda then said: You know what song Seymour always used to sing to me? It was Billy Joel. "Don't go changing, to try to please me. I don't want you to work that harrrrrd! I love you just the way you are." Turning to Seymour, Zelda exclaimed: Apparently not! It is a bunch of bull crap!

Seymour: Zelda is right you know. But, I have a solution. How about if we just stay the same? Or what if we take both "for better" and "for worse"? Sometimes we are better and sometimes we are a bit worse. It gives us a little flexibility.

Priest: First, you can't stay the same. Nobody ever stays the same. Impossible! With "better" or "worse," I can only do one or the other. If you want both "for better and for worse," you do not see a priest. You both have to go to a lawyer.

Seymour: A lawyer?

Zelda: That can be expensive. What are these lawyers going to do?

Priest: I can tell you. It is very complicated. The lawyers negotiate the terms of what exactly is better, and what exactly is worse. There can even be an arbitration clause that requires you both to arbitrate if one person is worse when that person is supposed to be better, or better when that person is supposed to be worse. With any dispute, you hire the lawyers all over again. It would cost you at least a couple hundred thousand dollars.

Seymour: We can't afford that. I will go with worse. It makes it so much easier.

Zelda: I will go with worse too.

Seymour: Zelda, what do you say. Let's not start this whole thing over with the "in sickness" or "in health." We will both go for "in sickness."

Zelda: You are such a smart man. I am feeling sick already! "In sickness" it is! I love you, Seymour!

Seymour: I love you too, Zelda!

This story shows how when two people are in love, they may not give much thought to "for better or for worse," or "in sickness or in health." The answer is always yes, but they are only focused on the "for better" and "in health" part. So, when I got married, I did put thought into this, and in particular, the problem of CrankaTsuris Menopause.

The deal I gave my bride, and the one she gave me, is that we both have to be "Normal" 75% of the time. However, we get to be "Crazy" 20% of the time, and "Insane" 5% of the time.

This is a great deal. If you lay out 300 days, this means you get to be completely insane on fifteen of those days, and you get two whole months of crazy.

Now, you may think this solution is a bit crazy, but hear me out. The problem is, people who are insane buy into the deal that they are required to be 100% normal, and they are not permitted to be insane. You see the problem here? If you are insane, but not allowed to be insane, you are left with one alternative. You have to convince your partner that you are not insane, and in fact, because your partner believes that you are insane, the only reasonable conclusion that you can come up with is that your partner is in fact insane. You partner, who up to this point, was not in fact insane, now goes insane because your partner has been accused of being insane when, in fact, you were insane all along.

Because of this, my counter-intuitive solution makes complete sense. You are feeling a bit insane, but that is okay. You are given permission. You are allowed 5% insanity. You are using up what you have been given. In fact, if you do not use it up, your insanity allowance would all go to a complete waste. Also, if we have used up our "Insanity quota," we can then start to dip into the 20% crazy allotment.

And, if one partner is a bit insane, or a bit crazy, it is always okay. Our marriage vows include both a bit of insanity and a bit of craziness, and of course, a whole bunch of normal. Just remember. By embracing the insanity and craziness, and not just trying to put it on each other, we find the solution to CrankaTsuris Menopause.

CHAPTER 8

HOPING FOR THE BEST
CRANKATSURIS

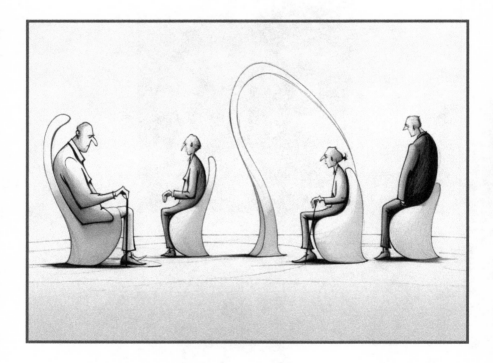

THERE IS ONE SAYING that never made a whole lot of sense to me.

"Hope for the best. But prepare for the worst."

Poor little Timmy never did well in school. He almost always failed his exams. When his parents asked him why he did so poorly in school, Timmy replied:

"I hoped for the best. But I prepared for the worst."

It turns out that this saying goes all the way back to Biblical times. The Jewish people were slaves in the land of Egypt. They worked to the point of exhaustion building the pyramids. However, one day, Aaron, who normally came home completely exhausted, was bounding with excited energy. He was holding a brochure in his hand.

"Miriam! Our days in Egypt are over. Look what Moses gave me."

Miriam looked at it and said: "It's a brochure. What's the big deal?"

Aaron replied, "It is not any brochure. Read it! 'Tired of Egypt in the winter? How about Israel in the spring? It is the Land of Milk and Honey. Time to take advantage of your new life living in the lap of luxury.'"

Miriam looked at it and started reading the small print. She looked at Aaron, and read the small print out loud: "Limit of Liability: While we expect to arrive in Israel in the spring, delays should be expected. Upon arrival, expect to be welcomed by a hostile population. Please be advised that by agreeing to go on this trip, you are waiving all rights to bring any legal action against Moses & Company and any of its affiliates. Be forewarned that while we do hope for the best, we will only be prepared for the worst."

Miriam then turned to Aaron and said: "I do not know about this. What does that mean? 'Only prepared for the worst.'"

Aaron quickly replied: "This is good. This means that they will be prepared for every problem, big or small. In other words, it means you can go on this trip without any worries, other than we will no longer be slaves in Egypt, and life in Israel will be filled with milk and honey."

All the Jewish households had similar conversations, and everyone signed the contract to go on the trip to the Land of Israel. They had been told that the departure time was 6:00 PM, but it turned out to be 6:00 AM. Everyone got out of bed, and half asleep, they packed up and began on their journey. The bread makers did not have time to let the dough rise, and the portable ovens could only manage to make crackers that tasted a bit like sawdust. When people complained to Moses, he turned to the people and said:

"We hoped for the best. But we only prepared for the worst."

They continued on their journey that appeared headed towards the Red Sea. The Egyptians were upset that the Jewish slaves were all leaving. Pharaoh sensed that letting these slaves leave would hurt him politically. More importantly, he saw that this upset his wife, who was still angry over losing their first born child that Moses had claimed responsibility for. Acting quickly, Pharaoh sent his army to go after the Jewish people and then return them back to the land of Egypt.

The Jewish people saw that they were approaching the Red Sea, and heard Pharaoh's army with their many chariots stampeding behind them. One of the leaders, Nathan, turned to Moses and asked:

"Now that you have taken us to the Red Sea, where are the boats to take us across? Surely, you would not have taken us on a journey straight to the Red Sea unless you had ready and waiting for us a beautiful giant cruise ship. Wasn't a cruise included in the trip? I went on a cruise once, and I can tell you this. The food was delicious. It was all you can eat and drink, no less! The entertainment was amazing. You think that I really care about this milk and honey. I signed up only just for the cruise. You know, your great great-great-great-grandfather Noah built a cruise ship. I heard it was amazing. They say that it even had a zoo on the ship. Can you imagine that!"

Moses shook his head and said to Nathan:

"There are no cruise ships. There are no small boats. There are no rafts. Not even a cardboard box to float across on. You see, as I said in the brochure, we were hoping for the best, but we only prepared for the worst."

Moses then looked up to the sky, and raised his staff and said:

"I hope for the best. I hope for the best. I hope for the best."

While the best would have been a beautiful luxurious cruise liner to go across the Red Sea, hoping for the best amazingly did cause the Red Sea to split and divide in half, allowing the Jewish people to walk across. Also, once the Egyptian army started going across, the water no longer parted, and the Egyptian army drowned trying to cross the Red Sea.

Once across the Red Sea, the Jewish people found themselves in the middle of the desert. It was hot in the desert, but the Jewish people were amazed when they came upon a beautiful mountain in the middle of the desert. Everyone wanted to go up the mountain where it was cooler. They were all very thirsty and hoped that by climbing the mountain they would find delicious mountain spring water. However, Moses told the people that they would have to stay down at the bottom of the mountain. He reminded them:

"While we hoped for the best, we only prepared for the worst. The worst is that you stay down here in the dry heat while I go up on special orders. It is even worse for me because I have problems with high altitudes. Also, I can tell you that the last time I was up there, there was this burning bush. The fire ruined my best toga outfit. And the burns. I still have the scars!"

The people were not happy, and Nathan told everybody not to worry. He explained:

"Look, I brought with me this giant golden calf. I got it specially made at the Idol Emporium in Pyramid City. We will throw a giant party with no social distancing, and we will all dance around this giant golden calf. That will help to take our minds off being stuck schvitzing at the bottom of the mountain in the middle of the desert."

Unfortunately, something was wrong with the giant golden calf. Anyone who got close to the calf came down with a mysterious virus. They named this virus Covid 1000BC. People were suffering, but they saw Moses coming down from the mountain, and they saw in him some newfound hope.

They all asked:

"Did you bring down a vaccine?"

"No vaccine but let me tell you. I got a bad cold climbing up and down the mountain. But I met with G–d and G–d gave me these two tablets with the Ten Commandments. These Ten Commandments will allow you to be better prepared and teach you how to hope for the best. However, with the vaccine, let me again remind you that while we hope for the best, we only prepared for the worst."

Unfortunately, the people who all touched the golden calf all did not survive, and the rest of the Jewish people continued on their journey. Spring time came and went, and it did not seem that they were anywhere close to getting to the Promised Land. Somebody was brave enough to ask Moses if he had brought a map with him so they would know how to get to the Land of Israel. Surely, he was smart enough to take a map with him.

Moses shook his head and said:

"I have no map. We were hoping for the best, but were only prepared for the worst."

Summer, autumn and winter came, and they were no closer to getting to the Land of Israel. The people were hungry, and thankfully, manna came from the sky and turned to food. The only foods that it turned into was borscht made out of cabbage and beets, cheese blintzes, and potato pancakes. For these three foods, there was an endless supply of sour cream.

Because the borscht was bright red in color, and the people finally got tired of eating borscht all the time, they began to use the borscht to create a bright red line in the sand as they made their way across the desert. For forty years, they were lost in the desert since they had only been going around in circles. Someone figured out that they could create the line of red borscht and the red line would mark off where they already had traveled.

With the red line marking where they had been, they would no longer have to go around the desert in circles anymore. The people gave a name for this line of borscht. They called it the "Borscht Belt."

The Jewish people finally reached the Promised Land, the Land of Israel, a land that in fact was flowing with milk and honey. However, as it was advertised in the brochure, the land had a population that was very hostile.

When the people saw that the land was already populated with the hostile population, they turned to Moses, and asked what to do. Moses, by now old and frail, turned to the people and said feebly, "We hoped for the best, but..."

Everyone shouted back.

"Enough! We know. We know already. Don't tell us. We only prepared for the worst."

Joshua then turned to the people and said:

"We have been wandering in the desert for forty years. Am I the only person who is a bit cranky?"

The people responded in unison: "NO! We are all cranky too!"

Joshua instructed the people:

"Now, we have to prepare for the best! So, this is what we will do. We will use our crankiness to let out the biggest CrankaTsuris. We have had forty years' worth of CrankaTsuris. We will unleash the forty years of CrankaTsuris, and all the hostile people will give us space to live in the Land of Milk and Honey."

The people unleashed a CrankaTsuris that was not heard on the planet since the days of the TyrantoCrankaTsuris. Joshua had thought that listening for forty years of CrankaTsuris would be too much for the hostile inhabitants. However, the hostile inhabitants were only hostile because they had their own CrankaTsuris. In fact, the hostile inhabitants were tired of listening to each other kvetching out their own worn-down CrankaTsuris.

So, when the Jewish people arrived with their own CrankaTsuris stories of surviving 40 years in the desert, the hostile inhabitants became very excited and threw the Jewish people a big party. The hostile inhabitants came with delicious cakes filled with milk and honey. The Jewish people were so moved by the welcome that they brought with them bottles of borscht, trays of cheese blintzes and potato pancakes, and lots of sour cream.

Apparently, talking amongst themselves and sharing CrankaTsuris stories, both peoples realized that they were living their lives, while they always hoped for the best, they always only prepared for the worst. That just led to lots of CrankaTsuris.

Afterwards, the elders got together and figured out how to always prepare for the best, and the land thrived really becoming the Land of Milk and Honey.

CHAPTER 9

CRANKATSURIS GURU

RECENTLY, THE SIERRA CLUB ORGANIZED A CLIMB up to the top of Mount Everest. This was to be a special climb up the revered mountain because all of the participants were among the top mountain climbers in the world.

Except for one.

Just before the group assembled to begin the ascent up the mountain, Mrs. Rosenblum walked up to the group with her wheelie bag and informed the leader of the group that she was joining the climb up the mountain.

The leader looked at Mrs. Rosenblum and saw that she appeared to be old and frail. He advised her how a strenuous and dangerous trip it would be to climb the world's tallest mountain, and she did not appear to be the kind of person who would be able to climb up to such heights.

Mrs. Rosenblum was undeterred. She looked the leader in the eye and said, "Let me tell you a bit about myself. I am alone now, but I was married to this bum for forty years. The bum left me, and you should know this. Being married to him was better training than any of your fancy shmancy mountain climbers may have ever had. Not even close."

The leader said "Okay. But you will need to sign a release. Also, because of your advanced age, I will have to assign you an extra Sherpa. The extra Sherpa will cost you double the price of one Sherpa. Maybe, you will need three. If you do not make it up, the Sherpas will have to carry you down."

Mrs. Rosenblum replied "I will sign any release you give me. But I do not need any of your Sherpas. Why don't you give the Sherpas to your fancy shmancy mountain climbers? They will need them more than I will. I assure you."

The leader shook his head in disbelief but now turned his attention to the entire group. He started to talk to the group:

"We are now going to ascend to the top of Mount Everest. You should all know that, at the top of the mountain, there is a cave. Inside the cave, there is a man who lives there who is known as "the guru." He is known as one of the wisest men in all the world, and leaders of countries and industry alike consult with him, seeking his guidance."

The leader continued:

"I have been informed that the guru has indicated that he is willing to meet only with the first person from our group to reach the top of the summit of the mountain. The one rule that the guru instructs that this person shall follow is that he or she is allowed only to speak three words. No more than three words! This will truly be a special experience for the first person to reach the top of the mountain."

The group of experienced mountain climbers and Mrs. Rosenblum, with her wheelie bag, began their ascent up the mountain. To the disbelief of all the other climbers, Mrs. Rosenblum outpaced everyone and was the first person to reach the top of the mountain.

When the leader arrived, he congratulated Mrs. Rosenblum.

"Mrs. Rosenblum, what you did was truly amazing. This is one of the most difficult climbs even for the most experienced mountain climber. As promised, since you were the first person to reach the top of the mountain, you, and only you, get a private meeting with the guru. But please remember. You can only say three words."

Mrs. Rosenblum walked inside the cave, and almost immediately, the other climbers outside the mountain heard lots of clanging, and the sound of glass being thrown and shattered against the wall of the cave. Everyone heard the distinct sound of a man shrieking, but nobody dared to venture inside the cave of the guru.

An hour later, Mrs. Rosenblum walked out of the cave. She looked at the leader and said, "Come to think of it, I will need two of the Sherpas to help your guru over here."

The leader, being white-faced and somewhat curious about what exactly happened inside the cave, asked Mrs. Rosenblum, "Did you say three words?"

Mrs. Rosenblum replied: "Yes. I said three words and only three words. Not a word more."

The leader asked: "What were the three words?"

Mrs. Rosenblum responded: "SHELDON, YOU PUTZ!"

As this story shows, because the CrankaTsuris is part of our true nature, sometimes we find ourselves climbing to the top of the highest mountain to get our fill of some good wholesome CrankaTsuris.

CHAPTER 10

CRANKATSURIS COOKING CLASS

IT IS FINALLY FRIDAY. You have made it to the end of the week. It is now the time to take a bit of CrankaTsuris inventory.

You started out the week determined to do a deep dive, but you have barely scratched the surface.

You wanted to start peeling the onion, but you were only given a sack of potatoes.

You needed to get to the heart of the problem, and you were told that "we are not doing brain surgery here."

You thought about taking the road less traveled, but you quickly discovered that there was no map.

You decided that you were going to start thinking outside the box, but you were facing a stack of boxes with the instructions that "there is a lot to unpack here."

You needed to turn over every stone, but it felt like being pelted with rocks.

By the end of the week, you resigned yourself to picking only the low hanging fruit, but most of that fruit had already spoiled and you found yourself staring at the delicious fruit just out of reach.

You were hoping that you would finally catch up, but you found yourself just dropping further down.

You were assured "not to worry because we will crack this nut," but you start to think that you are the only nut that will end up getting cracked.

We all have had one of these moments in our lives, and hopefully, this does not describe many days in your life, or a week in your life, or your entire life. NOOOO! But yes, be rest assured, we have all been there. There is a reason that they created the concept of "happy hour." There is a reason that we have TGIF chains spread throughout the country.

While I have enjoyed many happy hours in my life, and I am completely supportive of the "happy hour" concept, Effective Crankiness is more about doing something long lasting and positive rather than something that lands you in an Alcoholics Anonymous group, or with a bad hangover the next morning.

So, I am going to take you to the CrankaTsuris Cooking Class. Cooking is one of the great ways to treat a CrankaTsuris. You will never hear a great chef tell you how much he or she hates to cook. You never turn on the television to watch a cooking show to see someone in agony stuck in the kitchen. There are many books that talk about the "Joy of Cooking." But find me a single book that is titled "The Misery of Cooking." It just does not exist.

My mom was a fabulous cook, and she never complained a single day about the fact that she was cooking all the time. In fact, the only time that she actually complained was when we took her out to eat at the finest restaurant on Mother's Day. Her complaint was always the same.

"I can make the same food so much better!"

If ten people are reading this right now, half the people are thinking or saying "I do not know how to cook." I have had some people even tell me that they do not even know how to boil water.

For those people who do not know how to boil water, here is your first cooking lesson.

Take a pot. Add water. Place pot on stove over a medium or high flame. Wait about five minutes. When you see the water start to bubble, that means that the water is boiling.

See! You did it! That was easy.

For all of those other people who tell me that they can't cook, I still do not buy this. These people who tell me that they cannot cook are the same people who will bring home three dressers and a bookshelf from Ikea, and have everything assembled in twenty-five minutes. Because of this, I have to ask these people who say that they cannot cook one simple question:

"Can you read?"

If the answer is "yes," I can then explain to this person that "Add one cup of flour" means one thing. You have to add one cup of flour. Very simple.

For those people who are not able to read because they are watching TV all day, there are plenty of excellent YouTube videos you can watch.

Because you are reading this right now, I will assume that you can read, and I will start you on your path to cooking your CrankaTsuris away. I am not going to start with anything fancy. It is going to be simple, and easy to follow. You can even use prepared ingredients, and some frozen ingredients to put together with your fresh items.

I have a few rules here. It should be easy to whip up, taking you no more than an hour. It should taste delicious. It should be healthy. It should provide a beautiful and impressive display. It should be easy to clean up. It should leave you with a decent amount of leftovers that you can zap up in the microwave for the week.

Sounds good, right? Are you in? I can go into more complicated stuff where you get out your mini-chopper and your food processor.

That is not the point here. All I want is to get you on this path as a very effective and fulfilling way to deal with your weekly CrankaTsuris.

This is what you need:

A Cast Iron Pan, a Grill Pan, a Regular Frying Pan, Scissors for cutting meat or a good knife, a can of Extra Virgin Olive Oil Spray, and various seasonings that suit your own particular taste buds. I happen to be a big fan of Spiceology spices, but the ones you can get from a local supermarket can work out just fine.

We will be making the perfect butterflied roast chicken that is moist and delicious on the inside with the crispy skin on the outside. A four-pound chicken will take about 40 minutes.

For this, you preheat the oven to 450 degrees. Once it hits 450, take the cast iron pan, liberally spray it with olive oil, and season it with chicken seasoning, and let the pan heat in the oven for 30 minutes.

While the pan is heating in the oven, cut the chicken up the back, opposite from the breast side so the chicken opens up. Rinse it and pat it dry with a paper towel. Spray the chicken with your olive oil. Season it with your chicken seasoning, garlic powder, lemon pepper, paprika, and if you have a rosemary thyme seasoning, you can sprinkle that as well. Do this for both sides. Feel free to use paprika liberally on each side to your liking.

After the cast iron pan heats in the oven for 30 minutes, you can take it out, and then place the chicken flat on to the pan skin down. Listen to the sizzle. Just stick it into the oven. If it is close to 4 pounds, it stays in for 30 minutes. If it is a bit over 4 pounds, you can add 2 or 3 minutes depending on the size. I stay away from the 5-pound chickens just because they just do not taste as good and can be a bit tougher.

After 30 minutes, depending on the size of the chicken (for the 4-and-a-half-pound chick, add about 3 minutes), just flip it over so the skin side is now on top. Cook the chicken for another 10 minutes, and then take out the chicken. You are all done. Squeeze some lime on to the chicken and that will give it a nice citrus taste.

At the same time, we will be roasting on a separate pan fresh beets (you can peel them but I find that scrubbing them over water is easier and does the trick), small potatoes, brussel sprouts, multicolored baby carrots, fennel, Japanese or Indian baby eggplants (if you see them at your store), baby cauliflower, baby zucchinis, frozen or jarred artichoke hearts (drain oil).

We again spray the vegetables with the olive oil spray, and then season them to our liking. I use a Greek Freak seasoning on my potatoes, and brussel sprouts. I happen to like a pink peppercorn thyme seasoning on the other vegetables. You can season these the way you choose. It is your taste buds we have to satisfy here.

While the chicken is on the bottom rack of the oven, the vegetables can cook on top. The vegetables take about 45–50 minutes to roast. If I am cooking chicken at a 450 degree temperature, the 45 minutes will be fine. When I am not cooking chicken, I roast the vegetables at a 350 temperature and add about 10 minutes.

Separately, I like to do roasted asparagus. Again, after rinsing, I place them on a flat pan, spray some olive oil, and add seasoning to taste. I roast them for 10 minutes, regardless of the oven temperature.

On a grill pan, you can spray with olive oil, add low-sodium soy sauce or coco-aminos, and place any kind of mushrooms: shitake, baby bellas, oysters, portabellas, and add some sliced colored peppers.

This just needs about five to ten minutes to cook while you toss them over so they can brown on both sides.

Spray the frying pan with the oil, empty a bag of frozen spinach, then spray again with the olive oil. Sprinkle a bit of salt on to the spinach.

This should take no more than 5 minutes to get ready.

You need a soup too? How about a Tomato Red Pepper Corn Coconut Seafood Bisque?

I get the already prepared low-sodium Roasted Red Pepper Tomato Soup from the store. I also get a can of coconut milk. Of course, I get a bag of frozen seafood or giant scallops. Cod even works here quite well.

It all goes into a pot. I add chopped onion, chopped slivers of pepper, fresh or frozen corn, frozen peas, cumin to taste, curry powder to taste, and salt to taste. I stir and taste, stir and taste, and while I do this, I then decide a touch more of this or a touch more of that. At some point, I decide it is perfect. This also should be done after 30 minutes on a medium heat.

When you are done, add a big spoon of no-fat yogurt in your cup, and you will arrive in Soup Bisque Heaven. It is enough soup for a few days, and every day, the soup just gets better and better!!

Again, nothing should take longer than 30-40 minutes to cook, but an hour after you started, you will have a delicious chicken with many colorful vegetables, with an amazing soup. Lots of delicious leftovers. You can heat up some fresh bread and serve with a good wine. If you have some extra time, you can make a nice salad with pretty greens and some fruit added in.

Do you know what happens next? All that CrankaTsuris quickly melts away!!!

CHAPTER 11

CRANKATSURIS NOODLES

THIS IS A STORY THAT TAKES PLACE IN THE FUTURE. How far in the future, you may ask. I do not have a clue. However, I do hope it is not far into the future. Maybe, this is a story that is just around the corner because, as you know, we all need a good story to tell.

The air was always clean, and the sky was always blue. Everyone was always happy. This was possible because of one man. His name was Herbie Snoodleman. You see, Mr. Snoodleman, as he was referred to, was the inventor of the SnoodleMobile. Everyone drove around in their own SnoodleMobile, or just plain Snoodle, as it was affectionately called.

What made the Snoodle so special was that it was able to run only on noodles. All you had to do is put some noodles in the Snoodle, and off you would go. The delicious smell of noodles would fill the air. Not only that. You could add noodle sauce of your choice to the noodles in the Snoodle. When you arrived home from a long day at work, all you had to do was press the ejection button, and a fresh and delicious bowl of noodles and sauce would be ready to serve a family of four—just in time for dinner. Kids, in particular, loved the Macaroni Snoodle because it was able to make an amazing macaroni and cheese!

The SnoodleMobile was a big advance in technology that everyone appreciated. Before everyone drove around in their own Snoodle, they would get around in a KrautMobile. The KrautMobile ran on sauerkraut.

While the KrautMobile was very efficient, it was also very stinky. It was impossible not to have your clothes smell like sauerkraut by the time it was 10:00 AM. This was a big problem because it made everybody extremely cranky. No matter how many baths a person would take in a day, everybody smelled like sauerkraut. Everyone's clothes smelled like sauerkraut. Even the flowers in the spring would smell like sauerkraut!!

Because this made everyone irritable and cranky all the time, the world's greatest inventors tried to invent a car that did not run on sauerkraut. Everyone was unsuccessful until Herbie Snoodleman, or Mr. Snoodleman, as he was referred to, invented the SnoodleMobile.

With the success of the SnoodleMobile, Mr. Snoodleman was able to amass a great fortune. With this great fortune, not only did Mr.

Snoodleman open up many noodle shops, he also opened up the Snoodle Kidoodle Noodle Art Museum, which was the first art museum that focused solely on Noodle Art. Of course, the most prominent piece of Noodle artwork was a masterpiece created by the famous artist Noodle McDoodle. This work of art was titled *The Kidnoodle Lisa*.

Many people lined up for hours to see *The Kidnoodle Lisa*. Because of this, the Snoodle Kidoodle Noodle Art Museum quickly became the hottest ticket in town.

While everyone was in love with their Snoodle, and the Snoodle Kidoodle Noodle Art Museum, there was one person who was not happy at all. In fact, he was furious that people no longer wanted to drive around in a KrautMobile. This man, of course, was the inventor of the KrautMobile. His name was Sour Croodleman. Because nobody liked the KrautMobile anymore and nobody missed the smell of sauerkraut, everyone just referred to him as Stinky.

One day, Sour Croodleman decided that he would seek a bit of revenge on Mr. Snoodleman. He waited till the middle of the night. He then sneaked into the Snoodle Kidoodle Noodle Art Museum after hours when the museum was closed. When approached by security, Sour Croodleman sprayed the guards with his special Sauerkraut Spray, rendering them unconscious. Sour Croodleman then slowly walked up to *The Kidnoodle Lisa*. Sure enough, he opened up a special jar of Kimchi Sauerkraut and poured the jar all across *The Kidnoodle Lisa*.

The next day, Mr. Snoodleman discovered that his beloved piece of art, *The Kidnoodle Lisa*, had been covered with the Kimchi Sauerkraut. He was forced to close the museum because of the smell.

Mr. Snoodleman quickly took down *The Kidnoodle Lisa,* and wrapped it with a special noodle wrapping, and brought it over to the world's most prominent art restoration expert, Pierre Le'Toodle.

Pierre Le'Toodle spent weeks attempting to restore *The Kidnoodle Lisa*. Every day, Mr. Snoodleman would go to see whether Pierre Le'Toodle made any progress on restoring *The Kidnoodle Lisa*. When he was given a look at *The Kidnoodle Lisa*, he only had one thing to say:

"You have barely scratched the surface!"

Noodle McDoodle also was very concerned about how his most famous work of art had been damaged. He too went to see Pierre Le'Toodle on a daily basis just to inspect *The Kidnoodle Lisa*. When he was given a look at *The Kidnoodle Lisa*, he only had one thing to say:

"You have barely scratched the surface!"

Pierre Le'Toodle worked day and night, carefully scratching the surface, attempting to restore *The Kidnoodle Lisa*. Apparently, this worked with restoring other great works of art. He scratched so hard that, after a few weeks, he did not even have nails left on his hands. He thought if he kept scratching the surface, the sauerkraut stain and smell would go away. However, no matter how hard he worked scratching the surface, just before he went to bed at night, he would look at the painting and mutter to himself:

"I have barely scratched the surface!"

After he muttered about barely scratching the surface, he would always make sure to cover up *The Kidnoodle Lisa* with the special noodle wrapping. But one night, he was so tired, he simply fell asleep in his chair and left *The Kidnoodle Lisa* uncovered.

Pierre Le'Toodle owned a poodle named Schnoodle who would keep him company in his restoration studio. He had bought Schnoodle the Poodle when he still drove around in a KrautMobile. Schnoodle the Poodle loved the smell of sauerkraut so much, Pierre Le'Toodle started calling Schnoodle the Poodle "Wiener Schnoodle." When Pierre Le'Toodle's clothes started smelling like sauerkraut, Wiener Schnoodle would just roll his fur in the clothes and absorb all of the sauerkraut smell.

So, that night, after Pierre Le'Toodle was fast asleep, Wiener Schnoodle gleefully approached *The Kidnoodle Lisa* and started to fiercely lick the painting. He kept licking and licking until the sauerkraut smell and stain disappeared.

The next day, Pierre Le'Toodle woke up to find that *The Kidnoodle Lisa* was fully restored to its original beauty. He quickly called Mr. Snoodleman and Noodle McDoodle to come and see *The Kidnoodle Lisa*. They all celebrated with a big bowl of noodles.

Later that afternoon, the Snoodle Kidoodle Noodle Art Museum reopened, and *The Kidnoodle Lisa* was once again showcased as the finest example of Kidoodle Noodle Art.

A year later, Noodle McDoodle completed his next great work of art, and it was displayed alongside *The Kidnoodle Lisa*. He named it *The Kidoodle Noodle Poodle*.

Pierre Le'Toodle became an even more famous art restoration expert. He never merely scratched the surface ever again. Coincidentally, he renamed his art restoration company "Schnoodle Poodle and Le'Toodle Art Restoration."

And what became of Sour Croodleman, you ask? Because he learned that poodles loved sauerkraut, he opened his own Wiener Schnoodle Café!

It quickly became the hottest poodle spot in town!

CHAPTER 12

BARKING UP THE WRONG TREE CRANKA TSURIS

MANY YEARS AGO, when my daughter was growing up, we were lucky to have this amazing dog. His name was Albus Dumbledog. He must have come from another world because what made him so special was that he was a talking dog.

Yes. I owned a talking dog. We had some amazing conversations. I got to learn so much about dogs. He was also an amazing listener. I would come home from a bad day at work and tell him about all of my problems. When I asked him if it was okay to tell him all my complaints of the day, he would look at me with those understanding eyes, and he would always tell me the same thing:

"You are barking up the right tree, man!"

Unfortunately, I was never able to return the favor in the exact same way.

I would take Albus for long walks and every so often, he would see a squirrel or a cat running up a tree. Albus became excited, and hurriedly went up to the base of the tree and started barking. No matter how long he barked, the squirrel or the cat at the top of the tree would not come down. The squirrel was particularly mean, tossing nuts down at poor Albus.

Finally, I had to say:

"You are barking up the wrong tree, dog."

Albus was a very smart dog, and after being told that he was barking up the wrong tree, he went home and looked upon the internet exactly what type of tree had the best bark. Surely, he thought, if he figured out the type of tree that had the best bark, he then could be barking up the right tree.

After a few minutes of searching, Albus had his answer. It was an oak tree. Albus became very excited. He heard that on the other side of town next to a pond stood a giant oak tree. Finally, he thought, he could bark up the right tree.

I took Albus out for a walk the next day, and he made a special request. Albus never had made a special request before so I knew that this must be an important request.

"Papa. When you take me for a walk, can you take me by the giant oak tree on the other side of town?"

"Why?" I asked. What is so bad about peeing on any other tree in our neighborhood or on a hydrant like you normally do?"

"Papa. I do not want to pee on the oak tree. I just hear that the oak tree has this special bark. I just want to see it."

The very next morning, I drove Albus to the park that featured this oak tree. Sure enough, Albus noticed three squirrels and two cats crawling up the oak tree and started to bark like crazy. No matter how much Albus barked, the squirrels and the cats would not come down.

Finally, I had to tell Albus:

"You are barking up the wrong tree, dog."

Albus turned to me defiantly and said:

"Papa, I have the right tree. This is the tree with the best bark. I will keep on barking because I know I have the right tree!"

Albus kept barking and would not stop. People came from all the ends of the park to watch Albus bark. One person asked me:

"Does he always bark like this?"

I replied:

"Yes, but his bite is way worse than his bark."

The person who asked the question took one look at Albus' teeth. He quickly noticed that they were the biggest fangs he had ever witnessed on a dog. Terrified, and now knowing that Albus' bite is worse than his bark, he turned around and ran as fast he could in the opposite direction.

After a few hours of barking, Albus' voice began to get a bit hoarse, and his bark sounded more like a croak. The croak was so effective that hundreds of frogs from the pond nearby jumped out and surrounded Albus. With every croak from Albus, all the frogs danced around and formed a circle around Albus. Albus was delighted with his newly found frog fan club. The squirrels and the cats who had been hiding at the top of the oak tree came down to join in the fun.

I told Albus, chuckling, "Isn't it interesting. You barked up the wrong tree, but you croaked down the right pond."

This incident reminded me of another story. Our next-door neighbors were the Barker family: Woody and Maple Barker and their two kids, Birch and Willow. They were all the kindest and most generous neighbors on the block. If you needed any kind of help, you were sure that you could count on one of the Barkers to pitch in.

However, it was not always this way. In fact, they were the exact opposite. They were the meanest and stingiest people in town.

Apparently, the Barkers developed a severe case of Barking up the Wrong Tree syndrome. If one family member made any request to another, the answer was always the same:

"You are barking up the wrong tree."

If any neighbor asked for help, the answer was always the same.

"You are barking up the wrong tree."

Anyone who would walk by the house would hear the same commotion going on. One family member after another could be heard shouting:

"You are barking up the wrong tree."

Because of all the barking that the Barkers were doing, all of the Barkers lost their voices. All of a sudden, the house went completely silent.

The Barkers were terrified that they had lost their primary way of communication. The next day, they paid a visit to their primary physician.

The primary physician shook his head and told them that there was nothing that he could do. He told them:

"You are barking up the wrong tree."

The primary physician did come up with a suggestion.

"I recommend that you go see this family therapist. Her name is Dr. Sylvia Burt. She is a certified BURT therapist."

"What exactly is a BURT therapist?" Woody croaked.

"A BURT therapist specializes in teaching people how to bark up the right tree, and how to be the right tree to bark up. She is the best there is."

The Barkers went straight to see Dr. Burt. They practiced for weeks learning how to bark up the right tree, and to be the right tree to bark up. Once they mastered their newfound barking abilities, all of the Barkers' voices returned.

None of the Barkers ever barked up the wrong tree again.

Of course, our CrankaTsuris is our way of barking. If we find that we are always barking up the wrong tree, the CrankaTsuris gets worse and worse. These simple stories teach us the power we get when we finally can feel safe to bark up the right tree. This is the true essence of the CrankaTsuris Method.

CHAPTER 13

CrankaTsuris Chicken

MR. SCHLEMIEL WANTED TO RETIRE IN THE COUNTRY and live on a chicken farm, but felt that he could never afford it. It was his lifelong dream. He vigilantly checked the Chicken Farm Real Estate Magazine, and the prices were always way above what Mr. Schlemiel could afford.

But, one day, he was approached by Mr. Schmegeggi, who had heard about Mr. Schlemiel's dream to own a chicken farm, and he told Mr. Schlemiel that he had a chicken farm that was a tenth of the price of the average chicken farm.

Mr. Shlemiel could not believe his luck. "I'll take it!!" he exclaimed.

But, when Mr. Schlemiel got to the chicken farm, he immediately discovered that there were no chickens. Being very upset over this, he called Mr. Schmegeggi to complain.

"There's no chickens on the chicken farm!" Mr. Schlemiel cried.

Mr. Schmegeggi thought about this and said:

"You can't count your chickens until they hatch."

For a brief second, Mr. Schlemiel thought this made sense, and he screamed, "But there are no chickens to hatch because there are no chickens to lay eggs!!"

Mr. Schmegeggi thought about this and said:

"I thought you would say that so because I am such a nice guy, I went to the supermarket, and bought you two dozen eggs."

Mr. Schlemiel was not pleased. "I want chickens. Not an omelet!!" Where are the chickens?"

Mr. Schmegeggi pointed out of the window and said:

"The chickens crossed the road to get to the other side."

Mr. Schlemiel looked out the window and saw the other side with hundreds of chickens. He noticed that the grass was greener on the other side. So, Mr. Schlemiel complained:

"You never told me that the grass was greener on the other side!!!"

Mr. Schmegeggi quickly retorted:

"But the grass is always greener on the other side!!"

Mr. Schlemiel was fuming. "That's a paltry excuse if I ever heard one!!" Mr. Schmegeggi responded:

"Of course not. It is a poultry excuse."

As Mr. Schmegeggi continued to egg Mr. Schlemiel on, Mr. Schlemiel was in a very fowl mood indeed!!

CHAPTER 14

CRANKATSURIS SCHLEMIEL

AS YOU KNOW, Mr. Schlemiel is the person who bought the chicken farm from Mr. Schmegeggi. The only problem was that it had no chickens.

Now, this is the secret about Mr. Schlemiel. What makes Mr. Schlemiel so special is that he is one of those people that has lots and lots of Tsuris, but amazingly enough, he had never experienced CrankaTsuris.

The reason for this is quite simple. He just spends his entire life letting people take advantage of him, and he always just thought that was the way it always was. He just did not know any better.

But, one day, believe it or not, he woke up and thought to himself that today is a new day, and he said:

"I shouldn't let people take advantage of me. I am going to find a lawyer, the best lawyer, and I am going to sue those people who tried to take advantage of me. I'll show them, and nobody will dare take advantage of me again!!!"

So, Mr. Schlemiel found a lawyer, and the lawyer's name was Mr. Schmegeggi. Yes. This is the same Mr. Schmegeggi who sold Mr. Schlemiel the chicken farm. You see, Mr. Schlemiel really is a schlemiel.

Mr. Schmegeggi promised Mr. Schlemiel that when the case was over, nobody would ever mess with Mr. Schlemiel, and with the money he would get, Mr. Schlemiel would live a "Tsuris free" life.

The case proceeded to trial, and Mr. Schlemiel had a good case. We know this because Mr. Schlemiel was offered $5 million dollars to settle the case.

Mr. Schlemiel was very excited with the news, so excited in fact, that he went to Mr. Schmegeggi to take the money.

"Mr. Schmegeggi, please let's take the money. It's a lot of money, and I do not see $5 million every day. Remember, you said "Tsuris free"? This is it. Let's settle and go home!!!"

Mr. Schmegeggi was not moved. He replied:

"Mr. Schlemiel. The $5 million offer is an insult to my reputation. I will get you many times more than that. We will take the case to trial!!"

Mr. Schlemiel responded sheepishly:

"Ok."

So, the case went to trial. Apparently, it was not going too well. The jurors looked at Mr. Schlemiel with puzzled expressions and appeared openly hostile whenever Mr. Schmegeggi opened his mouth.

Still, Mr. Schlemiel was offered $3 million dollars to settle. Mr. Schlemiel, hearing this, ran over to Mr. Schmegeggi and pleaded:

"Mr. Schmegeggi, please let's take the money. I do not think the jurors like you very much, and they just look at me like I am some kind of schlemiel. I do not see $3 million every day. Please settle."

Mr. Schmegeggi looked at Mr. Schlemiel sternly, and said:

"Mr. Schlemiel. Trust me. No worries. I am the professional here. I plan to kill the jury with my closing argument!!"

Mr. Schlemiel responded sheepishly:

"Ok."

The closing argument did not go very well. It was clear that by the time they got to the closing argument, all of the jurors lost interest because they were all fast asleep. Still, Mr. Schlemiel was offered $1 million to settle.

Amazingly, Mr. Schlemiel was able to stay awake during the closing argument and he saw what was going on. He ran over to Mr. Schmegeggi and went down on his knees and begged:

"Mr. Schmegeggi. Please. Let's take the money. You said that your closing argument would be a killer, but I did not realize that would mean rendering them all unconscious. I do not see $1 million every day. Let's take the money!!!!"

Mr. Schmegeggi responded:

"I have a duty to protect the interests of my client, and the interest of my client is to take the case to verdict!!"

Mr. Schlemiel responded sheepishly:

"Ok."

The jury came back and awarded Mr. Schlemiel nothing. Zero. Verdict in favor of the defense.

It happens.

The next day, Mr. Schlemiel picked up the phone and asked for Mr. Schmegeggi. The receptionist picked up the phone and said:

"Oh. Mr. Schlemiel. Mr. Schmegeggi was very upset and very distraught over losing your case. He climbed to the top of the tallest building. He jumped off the top of the tallest building. Mr. Schmegeggi is dead."

Mr. Schlemiel responded:

"Ok."

The next day, Mr. Schlemiel again called and asked for Mr. Schmegeggi. The receptionist again answered the phone and explained:

"Mr. Schlemiel. Like I told you yesterday, Mr. Schmeggegi was very upset and very distraught over losing your case. He climbed to the top of the tallest building. Come to think of it, he probably took the elevator. The man was 100 pounds overweight, and I do not think he can walk up a flight of stairs. But he went to the top of the tallest building. He jumped off the top of the tallest building. Mr. Schmegeggi is dead."

Mr. Schlemiel responded:

"Ok."

The next day, again, Mr. Schlemiel picked up the phone and asked to speak to Mr. Schmegeggi. Once again, the receptionist answered, and politely explained:

"Mr. Schlemiel. Like I explained the last two days, Mr. Schmegeggi was very upset and very distraught over losing your case. He climbed to the top of the tallest building. He did not take the elevator. The elevator was out of service. But he climbed to the top of the tallest building. He jumped off the top of the tallest building. Mr. Schmegeggi is dead."

Mr. Schlemiel responded:

"Ok."

For the next week, Mr. Schlemiel continued to call, asking to speak to Mr. Schmegeggi. Finally, Mr. Schmegeggi's partner picked up the phone, exasperated, and said:

"Mr. Schlemiel. For the last ten days, you have called asking for Mr. Schmegeggi. And every day, we tell you the same thing. Mr. Schmegeggi was very upset and very distraught over losing your case. He climbed to the top of the tallest building. He jumped off the top of the tallest building. Mr. Schmegeggi is dead!!! Why do you keep calling?"

Mr. Schlemiel responded:

"I like to hear the story."

CHAPTER 15

CRANKATSURIS IMPATIENT

THERE ARE MANY DIFFERENT KINDS OF CRANKATSURISES that can easily take hold of us. Some can easily be dealt with. Others can be tricky, but many cures are available. However, probably one of the most difficult types of CrankaTsurises that we have all experienced is CrankaTsuris Impatience. The bus is late. When will this boring lecture end? "Timmy, are you dressed yet? We have to get to Grandma in an hour, and I do not want to be late!" "How long do we have to sit in this traffic?" "When can I open up my presents?"

CrankaTsuris Impatience is as natural to the human experience as CrankaTsuris itself. However, we have to be careful not to come down with a severe and terminal case of CrankaTsuris Impatience. Those who are afflicted with this extreme form of CrankaTsuris Impatience can never be in a relationship. They can never hold a job. They can never keep a project. They can never finish a book. The list goes on and on. It is not too off to say that this is a form of Attention Deficit Disorder. However, it has an added dose of CrankaTsuris for the person who is experiencing the impatience as well as those around that person.

Because of this, we have to look at those moments when we are feeling the CrankaTsuris Impatience as an opportunity to practice patience. There is a reason that we say "patience is a virtue." There is a reason that we like to complement ourselves once in a while by saying "My patience really paid off." The reason is that it is actually true. Once you start to see the opportunity, and then put it into practice, you can then notice the payoff.

You may ask where the "Patience pays off" line originated. The line "My Patience really paid off!" was made famous by one person. His name was Harry Bagrier. While that was, in fact, his real name, from the time he was a mere ten years old, his classmates would call him "Hairy Big Rear." Even his teachers would call him "Hairy Big Rear."

Poor Harry would try to correct those people who would call him that. However, it was of no use. He would constantly be called Hairy Big Rear. Unfortunately, Harry did have a big rear. Whether it was in fact hairy, nobody knew for sure.

Now, you can understand that if everyone always called you by a wrong name, and a mean one at that, you too would become quite impatient. You probably can understand how such a person can develop CrankaTsuris Impatience.

In fact, as Harry grew older, he developed a severe form of CrankaTsuris Impatience. He spent most of his day in his car, aggressively driving around and honking his horn. Harry loved to honk his horn at anything that disturbed him. He would just imagine that the person in front of him was one of those mean kids who would laugh at him and call him Hairy Big Rear.

Harry also used his car as his dining room. Harry never had the patience to actually sit at a table or go to a restaurant. So, he would always go to the nearest fast food drive-through and eat in the car. His car was littered with fast food cartons and paper wraps because Harry never had the patience to throw any of the wrappers away. If Harry had any passengers, which was very rare, they would literally have to climb on top of all the paper wrappers and open ketchup and mustard packages that were piled on to the front seat next to Harry.

Finally, one day, after honking at a person in front to him on the interstate, Harry was pulled over and arrested for being a public nuisance due to his aggressive and obnoxious driving. Harry was given a ticket. After he was found guilty, Harry was ordered to go before a judge for sentencing. The judge, by sheer coincidence, was named Judge Impatient.

Judge Impatient: Hairy Big Rear. Will you please stand up?

Harry: Your honor sir, my name is Harry Bagrier.

Judge Impatient: That is what I said. Hairy Big Rear. Please show your respect to the Court.

Harry: Yes, your honor. But it is Harry Bagrier.

Judge Impatient: I see that you have been found guilty of severe honking abuse while driving on the interstate. It is also noted that you had also been found guilty of honking your horn and causing a nuisance at McDonald's, Burger King, and Taco Bell. Hairy Big Rear, do you have an explanation for this continuing obnoxious honking?

Harry: Your honor. I am sorry, but you see, I happen to be a very impatient person. I can't stand to sit in traffic or wait online at the drive-through. The people in front of me are not paying attention to the road, but they are on their cell phones. So, I honk and honk, and honk till I can get their attention.

Judge Impatient: (Interrupted as he was busy texting on his cell phone) I missed the second part of your statement, but I heard that you have stated that you are a very impatient person. So, I will give you a choice. Either I will sentence you to three years in the State Penitentiary, or you can avoid a prison sentence altogether by spending some time at the Institute for Severely Impatient People.

Harry: If I go to the Institute, will it be on an inpatient or outpatient basis?

Judge Impatient: It will be on an inpatient basis. You will stay at the Institute until you learn to have some patience.

Harry: That is a problem. You see, I am very impatient. I do not think I can handle that inpatient stuff.

Judge Impatient: You have a choice. You can either be an inpatient or an in-prisoner. I recommend strongly that you go for inpatient. Other prisoners at the State Penitentiary do not treat hairy big rears all too well. You do not want me to go into any details.

Hearing this, Harry thought it would be wise to take the inpatient option. The next day, he packed up his bags, and drove off to the Institute for Severely Impatient People. He walked in and introduced himself to the Patient Team waiting for him at the door. The Patient Team was led by a tall silver haired man with a gray beard who, by sheer coincidence, had the name "Dr. Patience."

Dr. Patience: Harry Bagrier!! Welcome to the Institute of Severely Impatient People! You will at first find our treatment to be extremely difficult, but I can assure you. When you are permitted to leave, you will be a truly patient person.

Harry: You called me Harry Bagrier!

Dr. Patience: Yes. That is your name. We pay attention to details like that. Do you see the big sign above me on the wall?

Harry read the sign out loud: "Impatience creates tension. Just be patient and pay attention."

Dr. Patience: Yes. That is the practice. Now, your first task after you check in to your room is to come back down and clean your car. We noticed that your car is filled with wrappers and cartons from all the fast food stops in town. You will fold the wrappers and stack them in a neat pile. The plastic cups all have to be stacked as well. When you are done, you can come back to the Institute for the next assignment.

Harry: You called me Harry Bagrier. Nobody has ever called me by my real name before. But, cleaning out my car can take hours. There are years and years of wrappers in there. Some are stuck together by old ketchup and mayonnaise packages.

Dr. Patience: Harry, just be patient and pay attention. Impatience creates tension. Do you want to know what that tension will be if you show impatience?

Harry feebly asked, "What is the tension?"

Dr. Patience answered: "The State Penitentiary."

Harry did not want to go to the State Penitentiary. So, Harry then went to his car. One by one, he pulled out each wrapper, each condiment package, and all the plastic cups that took up all of the passenger seats in the car. Dr. Patience had his staff bring over three recycling dumpsters that were completely filled up by the time Harry was all finished. Harry felt a sense of pride that he actually was able to see the inside of his car.

That night, he was led to the kitchen. The staff was beginning to prepare a delicious meal with all the finest ingredients. Harry's appetite grew from the smell. The chef walked over to Harry with a peeler. The chef's name, by sheer coincidence, was Chef Patience.

Chef Patience: Tonight, we will have a delicious feast. But first, we have to prepare the meal. You will have the job of peeling. Peeling potatoes. Peeling onions. Peeling beets. Peeling zucchini. Peeling apples. Peeling mangos. Do you understand? Remember. Show patience and just pay attention. Be impatient, and you will create tension.

Harry feebly asked, "What is the tension?"

Chef Patience answered, "The State Penitentiary."

Harry did not want to go the State Penitentiary. So, Harry began to peel the pile of vegetables and fruits that was placed before him. That night, he was amazed by how delicious everything tasted. He was also touched by the fact that everyone called him Harry. There was not a single person who referred to him as "Hairy Big Rear."

The next day, Harry was led into a large room that was completely bare except for the cushions and mats placed side by side. The walls were painted white. There was a window that allowed the light to shine through. He was welcomed by a gray-haired man with a silver beard. Harry was told that this man was known as a "Zen Master." The Zen Master's name, by sheer coincidence, was Master Patience.

Master Patience: Harry Bagrier. So nice to meet you. For the next seven days, you will be sitting on a cushion with our other guests, and simply meditate or stare at the wall. You will sit for 30 minutes, and when the bell rings, you will do a walking meditation for another 10 minutes. We will do this all day. You will keep your eyes open and count from one to ten, and then count backwards from ten to one. Remember to just be patient and pay attention to your counting practice. Be impatient, and you will create tension.

Harry feebly asked, "What is the tension?"

Master Patience answered, "The State Penitentiary."

Harry did not want to go to the State Penitentiary. So, Harry sat on the cushion and began to count one to ten, and then ten to one. Over and over again, he counted, until he felt he was in a trance. At the end of the sitting meditation, everyone walked slowly in a meditative pace. When everyone was done, they all walked up to Harry and bowed, and stated his name.

"Harry Bagrier."

Harry was touched that everyone called him Harry. Harry also began to feel a sense of peace and calm. At the end of the seven-day meditation, everyone walked over to Harry and bowed. When they all bowed, they each said respectfully:

"Master Harry Bagrier."

The next day, Harry was met by Dr. Patience. Harry was excited to see Dr. Patience because he thought that, after the seven days of meditation, he would be allowed to leave the Institute. Dr. Patience, however, was holding a very large pill. Next to him, there was a man holding a straightjacket. A nurse was holding a spoon and a glass of water.

Dr. Patience: Harry, you have done well so far. All you have to do is swallow this pill. Once you swallow the pill, we will pronounce you as being fully cured, and you will be released. You get one attempt now to swallow the pill. If you fail, we will then put you in a straightjacket. Your task will then be to get out of the straightjacket and place the pill in the spoon. You then put the pill into the glass of water, and drink the water. You complete that task and you will be released. Remember just to be patient and pay attention. Show impatience, and you will create tension.

Harry asked feebly, "What is the tension?"

Dr. Patience answered, "The State Penitentiary."

Harry did not want to go to the State Penitentiary. Harry quickly grabbed the pill from Dr. Patience's hand and tried to swallow the pill. However, no matter what he did, Harry found that the pill was just too hard to swallow. Harry was then led to a room and put into the straightjacket. The spoon and glass were placed on the table at the end of the room.

At first, Harry started to wrestle and thrash back and forth trying to squeeze out of the straightjacket. After a few hours, Harry got tired and plopped to the floor. He felt his breath, and just started to stare at the spoon with the pill. Harry became transfixed by the spoon, and after an hour of staring at the spoon, the spoon began to levitate off the table. Harry intuitively began to look at the spoon as if he was giving it directions. The spoon plopped the pill into the glass of water, and the pill quickly dissolved.

Harry then noticed his arms beginning to move. Slowly, he was able to move the left arm out of his left sleeve, and then saw that he was able to do the same with his right arm. Once his arms were both free, he lifted the straightjacket off. Harry walked over and drank the water.

Harry Bagrier was declared to be a patient person and was released from the Institute for Severely Impatient People. Years later, Harry no longer had a big rear. He changed his name to Sammy Spoodini. He became known as a Master Magician and was able to be placed in a straightjacket and chains, put into a big trunk, dropped into a giant pool of water, and still escape alive. He also opened up the finest restaurant in town called "Spoodini's Great Feast."

When asked about his success, Harry had only one thing to say:

"Patience really pays off."

CHAPTER 16

DILLY DALLY WILLY NILLY CRANKATSURIS

DILLY DALLY WILLY NILLY CRANKATSURIS is one of the more peculiar kinds of CrankaTsuris. This is because there are so many different variations of this CrankaTsuris. You can go only with a Dilly Dally, or a Willy Nilly, or you can combine the two to have a Dilly Dally Willy Nilly CrankaTsuris. Many couples can have an arrangement in which one person does the Dilly Dally and the other person goes Willy Nilly. They can take turns and switch roles. It does not matter who chooses what, but it is guaranteed that it will leave the couple with an extended CrankaTsuris.

I have personally experienced the Dilly Dally Willy Nilly CrankaTsuris whenever I have returned home from the Ikea Furniture Store and splurged on a few "easy to assemble" furniture items. I open up the box of pieces of wood planks, an assortment of metal and plastic screws, and the easy-to-follow instructions. I assume that they are easy to follow because they decided that it was so easy they would not need to include actual words. All that was needed were badly drawn pictures.

They also include a list of parts with the picture of each part. Even though they have thirty-seven screws of different sizes, when I try to line up the screws next to the wooden planks, they all seem to be very close in size. Also, it always seems to me that the package has one screw missing.

At that point, I go into a special box I keep exactly for this situation. It is a called the "extra screws" box that they have shelved at Ikea right by the cash register as you are about to check out. I always make sure to buy a couple of these extra screw boxes just in case.

You can never have too many screws, I think to myself.

This is when I start to dilly dally. I look at the pictures. I look at the pieces of wood and screws that I nicely assorted. I look again at the pictures. I look again at the floor covered with my future bedroom dresser. Did I mention that I have not even started to open the boxes that contain the pieces of nightstand. I start to think to myself, *Hey, I also bought a lamp. I can put the lamp together. That can't be so hard.* Of course, I then remember that I forgot to buy light bulbs. I then take a deep breath and just decide to go for it. I will put together the dresser. I spent two hours just organizing the parts. I should just now get to work.

Sure enough, nothing goes smoothly. I have a difficult time figuring out the difference between the pieces for the left side and the right side, the pieces for the front and the back, and the pieces for top and the bottom. They all look so alike to me. Eventually, I do not really figure it all out, but just decide for myself that it just doesn't really matter. They all look alike so each piece must be interchangeable. It will all work out in the long run. I start to screw in the planks of wood together.

Of course, the screws do not always screw all the way in. I screw and screw and screw till the screw loses its ability to get screwed, and I can see that it is still only halfway in. I then decide that if a screwdriver no longer works, certainly, a hammer will, and I begin to hammer in the screw. While I actually succeeded in hammering the screw into the plank of wood, I realize shortly afterwards that I picked the wrong plank of wood, and used the wrong screw. I also learned that after you hammer in a screw, there is no real way to get the screw back out. The screw had lost its groove.

After five hours of doing the Dilly Dally and Willy Nilly, I experienced the Dilly Dally Willy Nilly CrankaTsuris. The sound I made with the hammer is the feeling I now experience in my head. At that point, I was able to find a cure for my Dilly Dally Willy Nilly CrankaTsuris. I took a couple of Tylenol pills, opened up a can of beer, and called up Ikea to make an appointment with an Ikea engineer. They sent over this engineer the very next day. He presented with me with his documents which included his PhD in engineering, and the Nobel Peace Prize he won for writing the Ikea Furniture Assembly Manual.

Within an hour, to my astonishment, all of my bedroom furniture was completely assembled. It was almost all perfect. Because of the Willy Nilly hammering performance from the day before, I had to settle for a two drawer dresser instead of three. I decided that this was well worth the price for resolving my Dilly Dally Willy Nilly CrankaTsuris.

As I mentioned earlier, many couples perfect the Dilly Dally Willy Nilly CrankaTsuris as if it is a dance they will perform at an episode of Dancing with the Stars. One partner has perfected the Dilly Dally. Day after day, the other person, who makes up the other side of this fine pair, gets to witness his or her partner perfecting the Dilly Dally.

It has in fact been perfected. Partner One has so perfected this Dilly Dally that Partner One obtained a patent, copyright, and a trademark for this particular Dilly Dally. Partner One believes that they have the sole and exclusive right to this particular Dilly Dally that took decades to perfect.

After a while, Partner Two finds that Partner One's Dilly Dally is getting a bit old, and quite frankly, it is becoming quite annoying. Without warning, Partner Two decides to unleash a Willy Nilly CrankaTsuris. By the way, Partner Two also believes that this particular Willy Nilly has a patent, copyright, and a trademark, which gives Partner Two an exclusive right to unleash at a moment's notice.

Partner One gets completely startled and upset because the Dilly Dally has been disrupted. Partner One has perfected this Dilly Dally so it is taken as a violation. The couple then begins their shouting match which is the Dilly Dally Willy Nilly CrankaTsuris.

After they go through the first phase, Partner Two wins the battle, but not the war. Partner One agrees to temporarily suspend the Dilly Dally. Partner Two, at first, is pleased, but then quickly sees that Partner One got up from the Dilly Dally Couch, and started to do all the things that Partner Two had a fantasy that, one day, Partner One would actually do. However, Partner Two quickly realizes that Partner One is doing everything Willy Nilly. Partner Two finds Partner One's Willy Nilly even worse than the Dilly Dally.

Out of frustration, Partner Two tells Partner One:

"You know what. Why don't you go back to your Dilly Dally? At least I was used to it. I just can't take your Willy Nilly."

Partner One, with great relief, goes back to that old Dilly Dally. The war has been won.

Of course, years later, Partner Two learns to do their own Dilly Dally. As they say, if you can't beat them, join them.

But the dance does not end there. Partner One does not know how to experience the Dilly Dally of Partner Two. Because it is so foreign, Partner One decides to go Willy Nilly.

And that is how the dance continues.

It turns out that children invented the Dilly Dally Willy Nilly CrankaTsuris. Once upon a time, there was a mother of twin kids. The mother's name was Nervous Nelly. The son was named "Willy Nilly," and the daughter was given the name "Dilly Dally."

Of course, Willy Nilly would do everything Willy Nilly. Dilly Dally would spend all day just Dillying and Dallying.

When they were just toddlers, when food was placed on their plates, Willy Nilly would toss the food all over the room. Barely any of the food would reach Willy Nilly's mouth. Dilly Dally was not much better. Food was cut up and rolled into balls or turned into a mush. Dilly Dally would then let out a CrankaTsuris protesting the mush she created on her plate.

A few years later, when Nervous Nelly instructed Willy Nilly and Dilly Dally to clean their rooms, Willy Nilly would just toss all of his clothes into a closet until it was one big pile. It became impossible to tell the difference between the clean and dirty laundry.

This was slightly better than Dilly Dally. Dilly Dally never cleaned her room. She just couldn't get herself going. Because of this, you can never see the bedroom floor. Every inch was just completely covered by her clothes.

In school, it was even worse. Both Willy Nilly and Dilly Dally took their final exams. They both scored a zero on their exams. Because the tests were all in multiple choice, nobody ever scored a zero before. Nervous Nellie was called to come into school with both Willy Nilly and Dilly Dally and they met in the principal's office.

Principal: Before we decide on a plan for these two youngsters, I want to hear an explanation from both of them how they managed to score a zero. A monkey could not get a zero on these exams. Yet, both Willy Nilly and Dilly Dally somehow managed to get not a single question correct.

Willy Nilly went first.

Willy Nilly: It is all very simple. The tests ask a question and then said that one of the four choices would be correct. So, I just decided to pick all four. If one of the four is the correct answer, I thought I would be guaranteed getting the answer right if I just picked all four choices. Unless all four choices were incorrect, I believe I should be getting an A-plus for scoring 100%!

Principal: It does not work that way. The test measures what you have learned. And you, Dilly Dally. You just turned in an exam that was completely blank. You did not answer a single question.

Dilly Dally: Principal. I can assure you that it was based on both moral and logical principles. I figured that everyone studied for the exam right. But, with every question, when the choices are A, B, C, or D, somebody would pick A. Another few students would pick B. Others may pick C or D. If I picked A as my answer, I am saying that everyone, who picked B, C, or D, are wrong, and I think that it is just not fair to them.

Willy Nilly: That makes complete sense to me. If the teacher decides the correct answer is A, but if six out of ten students gave B as the answer, that says fifty percent of the class believes B is the correct answer. If fifty percent believe B is the right answer, maybe the right answer is B.

Principle: That would be sixty percent. Six out of ten is sixty percent.

Willy Nilly: Not if four out of ten say it is fifty percent. If four out of ten say fifty percent, this would then mean that eighty percent believe it is fifty percent.

Dilly Dally: Willy Nilly! You are so smart!! I would have just dilly dallied trying to figure that one out.

Nervous Nellie: Can you understand why these two make me so nervous? And they are our future! What will become of this world! We are doomed, I tell you. Doomed! Principal, you have to come up with a solution. The survival of all of humanity is at stake!!

Principal: I see what you are saying. It turns out that we have a special Institute on the other side of town that specializes with severe cases of Willy Nilly and Dilly Dally. They will have to stay at the Institute, but I can guarantee you this. The Institute has a high success rate. Also, because the future and survival of all of humanity is at stake, I believe both Willy Nilly and Dilly Dally will qualify for a scholarship.

At the Institute, Willy Nilly and Dilly Dally was given puzzles to put together, each one more difficult than the next. They were then given Lego sets, and they ended up creating their own miniature Lego Land. They had to cook their own food, following the recipes of many famous chefs. They were given their own chemistry sets, and they were then taught how to make their own medicine.

When Willy Nilly and Dilly Dally left the Institute, they were no longer Willy Nilly and Dilly Dally. Nervous Nelly was no longer nervous because it turned out that all of humanity was saved.

This is where I share a story a friend told me about her dad, and I would only do it justice if I used her own words:

My dad grew up in a one room apartment living on public assistance.

He collected comic books and sold them.

With the money he earned, he bought a chemistry set. He was ten years old at the time.

He blew a hole in the ceiling of his apartment with the chemistry set.

A passion, as well as various parts of the apartment, was ignited.

In high school, a chemistry teacher took interest in his future.

She helped him get a full scholarship to college.

He studied chemistry and engineering.

Growing up, money was tight in my family. I always wore my cousin's old clothes which always fit kind of funny.

When I was in 5th grade, my dad started a chemical engineering company.

Money was REALLY tight.

By 9th grade, his company was building some of the largest pharmaceutical plants in the country.

I didn't have to wear my cousin's clothes anymore.

My dad, however, wore his old clothes. From the 1970s. He looked like John Travolta in shirts that had taken one too many spins on the disco floor.

He would wear shirts until they fell apart.

He had only one credit card. For emergencies.

He carried around a wad of cash in a rubber band.

Not a regular rubber band. A broccoli rubber band from the supermarket.

He wouldn't waste work supplies.

We begged him to get a wallet. A money clip. Anything.

He wouldn't. The broccoli rubber band worked. His old clothes worked. Don't get me started on cars.

I used to say, "Dad, you can have any kind of car you want! What kind of car do you want?"

"A blue car," he replied.

By the time that he had died, he had built pharmaceutical plants around the world.

He even treated himself to a blue car, paid for in cash, just like his new house.

"If you can't buy it in cash, don't buy it," he would say.

He didn't spend beyond what was tucked into that broccoli rubber band.

My teacher and mentor, Roshi Enkio Pat O'Hara, who runs the Village Zendo in Greenwich Village in New York City, would give dharma talks on Sunday mornings and at silent meditation retreats and always remind us of "utilizing skillful means." When you utilize skillful means, there's not much room for willy nilly or dilly dally. And then, when you learn to do that, you have found the cure for Dilly Dally Willy Nilly CrankaTsuris.

Just like my friend's dad did.

CHAPTER 17

SPINNING YOUR WHEEL CRANKATSURIS

SPINNING YOUR WHEEL CRANKATSURIS is one form of CrankaTsuris that everybody experiences at one time or another. You start by setting the wheel in motion. After a while, you notice that the wheel is spinning faster and faster. However, you are not moving at all. You have convinced yourself that you are stuck in the mud.

Typically, this is a moment when you feel that you are all alone. This is rather convenient because you also have the feeling that you want to scream. If you are not alone, there is someone else in the car stepping on the gas pedal. You desperately push and push to get the car out of the mud, and your only success is now having yourself covered in the mud that had been flying at you for the last ten minutes. The wheel is still spinning, but the wheel is now buried even further in the mud than before.

Spinning Your Wheel CrankaTsuris is an important CrankaTsuris to examine because this particular feeling can be one of hopelessness. However, if we look at this particular CrankaTsuris closely, sometimes we can actually see that there is much more hope than there is hopelessness when we are afflicted with this particular form of CrankaTsuris.

This lesson can be seen in the classic movie *The Wizard of Oz*. Or, at least the way I retell the story of *The Wizard of Oz*. Because we all know the original story, my version starts a bit after Dorothy and the Gang's first trip to see the Wizard. The Scarecrow wanted a brain. The Tin Man wanted a heart. The Cowardly Lion wanted courage. And, of course, Dorothy just wanted to go home to Kansas.

Believe it or not, the Wizard did not give them a single thing that they had asked for. Inexplicably, this supposedly wonderful wizard just sent them out to the Wicked Witch's castle to bring back the broom of the Wicked Witch of the West. Why did the Wizard need a broom? I do not have a clue. He probably could have just sent one of his assistants to the hardware store for a brand-new broom.

The Wizard also requested a bucket of the Wicked Witch's World-Famous Wicked Wings. This bizarre request to get a broom and a bucket of chicken wings (surely to be cold by the time they got back to the Wizard's castle), of course, was not an easy lift since we know that Dorothy had previously killed the Wicked Witch's sister in what was called a freakish accident. Even if Dorothy was innocent, the Wicked Witch was still awfully wicked. Surely, the Wicked Witch would want some pay-back revenge for her equally wicked, but now dead, sister.

Of course, as expected, Dorothy got abducted by the Wicked Witch. The Wicked Witch gleefully cackled taunts at poor Dorothy sitting in the castle dungeon, "You are going to die!!" Fortunately, the Scarecrow, the Tin Man, and the Cowardly Lion, by showing smarts, a lot of heart, and tremendous bravery, successfully snuck into the heavily guarded castle, and freed Dorothy from a certain death. Unbelievably, they melted the Wicked Witch with a bucket of water.

The Wicked Witch quickly disintegrated and was no more. The guards were overjoyed, and gave Dorothy the Wicked Witch's broom. One guard then ran into the kitchen, and whipped up a fresh batch of the Wicked Witch's Wicked Wings. Another grateful guard presented them with a box of those delicious Munchkin Land Muffins. One little secret here to tell you. They happen to be made with real Munchkins! The Wicked Witch was not called the Wicked Witch for nothing.

Everybody in the castle were then so happy and overjoyed by the death of the Wicked Witch, they all busted into song. We all know that they were overjoyed and happy simply by hearing the first two words of the song. "Ding Dong!" I can tell you that whenever I have had a moment in my life when I was so overjoyed, the first words that always popped in my head were "Ding Dong!" Perhaps, you have had that exact same experience.

After finishing singing the Ding Dong song, Dorothy and her friends eagerly went quickly back to see the great Wizard of Oz. With the broom, the bucket of the Wicked Witch's Wicked Wings, and the Munchkin Land Muffins, surely now the Scarecrow was going to get a brain, the Tin Man was going to get a heart, the Cowardly Lion was going to receive courage, and most importantly, Dorothy was going back home to Kansas to be with Auntie Em.

After knocking on the Palace Door, the guard let everyone in. The guard then instructed them to all wait in a room while he brought to the Wizard the broom, the bucket of the Wicked Witch's Wicked Wings, and the box of Munchkin Land Muffins. After a few hours pass, they are led into the Grand Hall where the Wizard was sitting.

The Wizard then began to speak. "These Wicked Wings are the best. I want you all to go back to the castle and get me the recipe. Just think! If I get a hold of the recipe for these Wicked Wings, I can open up Wicked Witch's Wicked Wing shops all throughout Emerald City. I won't have to do this dumb Wizard gig anymore.

I'll tell you what. You get me the recipe, and you will all get a ten percent cut in the profits. What do you say?"

The Scarecrow folded his arms. "I say no way!! We had a deal! We brought you what you asked for, and I want a brain."

Tin Man shouted, "I want a heart!"

The Cowardly Lion stuck his head in. "I want some courage!"

And Dorothy, holding her dog Toto, said: "And, I just want to go home!"

The Scarecrow then walked up to the Wizard and started to speak. "I know exactly the kind of brain I want too. Last week, I saw this movie. I think it was called *Young Frankenstein*. They put in this big man's head a "More-On" brain. That is what I want! A More-On brain."

Tin Man turned to Scarecrow. "I saw the movie too. I think that it really was a Moron brain that they ended up putting in the monster's head. You definitely do not want that."

"Thank you, Tin Man," Scarecrow replied. "Okay. Wizard, give me one of your Less-On brains!"

The Wizard shook his head. "Unfortunately, I do not have any brains handy right now. There is a ten-year waiting list even for a Moron brain. However, I do have something for you. Where I come from, there are people no less brainless than you are. However, they get their parents to pay huge sums of money to go to a place called University. There, for four years, they barely learn a thing, but they get to party, drink lots of alcohol, and take all sorts of drugs. I hear they end up killing any brain cells they had in their head to begin with. When they finally get out, they get this piece of paper called a diploma. So, it now gives me the distinct honor and pleasure to present to you, Scarecrow, with a diploma from Emerald City Technical College."

Scarecrow looked at his diploma. "It says 'Bachelor of Science: Straw Maintenance.' Hey! This is not our deal. You are spinning my wheel!"

The Tin Man then turned and said, "What about me? I want my heart. Surely, there can't be a waiting period for a heart transplant!"

"Let me think." said the Wizard. "Can I offer you some Wicked Wings while I figure out what to do?"

"No. Thank you," said the Tin Man "To be honest with you, Wizard, the Wicked Wings give me a bit of heartburn."

The Wizard then waved his hand. "No problem. Now, I know what I can do. Check out this old-fashioned alarm clock. Shaped and colored just like a heart no less! Stick it in that tin can of a body of yours, and it will sound just like the real thing!"

"Are you kidding me?" said the Tin Man in disbelief. "Look at my wrist? I am wearing an Apple Watch!! I did not risk my life to get a stupid cheap plastic two-dollar alarm clock! This is not our deal! You are spinning my wheel!"

Cowardly Lion then turned to the Wizard. "What about me? I need to get courage, and I know exactly what I need to get it! My three older brothers always tell me the same thing. They say that I need to grow a pair!"

The Wizard looked puzzled. "A pair of what? You want me to grow you a pear tree?"

The Cowardly Lion replied, "No. Not a pear tree. I do not know exactly what they are, but my brothers tell me that they are called 'cajoles.'"

The Wizard again waved his hand dismissively. "I have never heard of them. But this is what I can do. For your bravery and skill in taking care of getting rid of the Wicked Witch, I proudly present you with the Metal of Courage."

The Cowardly Lion looked at his metal. "I can see the word 'Courage' on the front. I can't make out what it says in the back."

The Scarecrow took the metal and read aloud. "It says 'There are no losers in life. Everyone is a winner! You are the last winner!' You are the last winner? I do not think that is much of a compliment."

The Cowardly Lion was angry. "I do not like this. This is not our deal. You are spinning my wheel!"

Dorothy looked down. "I guess this means that you can't help me either." said Dorothy.

The Wizard again waived his arm. "Absolutely false. For you, I plan to take you home personally in my hot air balloon that brought me here thirty years ago. Of course, I haven't flown it in thirty years, but I am sure that it is like riding a bike!"

Tin Man looked sternly at Dorothy. "He is spinning your wheel too!"

"That is right!" added the Scarecrow. "Don't you remember what Auntie Em use to tell you? She said "Never take a hot air balloon ride with strangers." It can be around the world in eighty days with this lunatic! A fourteen-year-old girl in a hot air balloon with a strange old man does not sit right with me! And, it does not even have a pot to piss in!"

The Tin Man looked at his watch. "Perhaps, I can use my Apple Watch to just order you an Uber to get back home. Of course, that is, if I ever can get internet here!"

Then suddenly out of nowhere, the Cowardly Lion leaped towards the Wizard. With one big bite, he swallowed the Wizard whole. The Wizard was no more.

The Scarecrow turned to the Lion. "That was amazing! And look at Lion! Lion, you just grew a pair!!"

Everyone joyfully yelled, "Cajoles!!"

The Lion then beamed proudly: "Ain't it the truth! Ain't it the truth!"

With the brave Lion and his cajoles now by their side, the Scarecrow was then able to get a brain. The Tin Man got his heart. Dorothy got limousine service back to Kansas. They all lived happily ever after.

Of course, the point of the story is that they had thought they needed to see the Wizard to get what they already had. The Wizard was more of a distraction, and caused all of them to think that they were just spinning their wheel.

This brings me to an important story that a Rabbi shared with my class when I was a boy. The Rabbi said he had asked another class the question "What is the most important thing for a human being to experience in life?"

One boy quickly answered "pleasure!"

Everyone looked at the boy as if he was going to get in trouble with the Rabbi. However, the Rabbi told everyone that the little boy's answer was actually the correct one. The Rabbi then asked, "What is the opposite of pleasure?"

The same little boy responded quickly. "Pain!" he said.

The Rabbi nodded his head. This was incorrect. The Rabbi said that the correct answer to this question was "comfort." Everybody looked puzzled by this answer.

"Pleasure," he explained, "is sometimes realized after much hard work, sacrifice, and even pain. Think of the championship basketball team, the person that climbs Mount Everest, or the person who just finished running their first marathon. Or just think of the most painful thing there is. Giving birth. 'Comfort' however, is for the person who just never got out of bed. And, of course, if everyone was comfortable, nobody would be left because of the giving birth problem."

"Ding Dong!" The alarm rings. It is now time to get up.

And with this thought in mind, perhaps we have found a way to deal with Spinning Your Wheel CrankaTsuris.

CHAPTER 18

CRANKATSURIS KUGEL

"SHIVA" IS THE JEWISH WORD for the seven-day period of mourning that a Jewish person has to do after the passing of a loved one. During this seven-day period, family members and friends gather at the house of the deceased, and spend the time mostly eating, but also telling the CrankaTsuris stories of the person who had just passed away.

We learn that these stories are true CrankaTsuris stories because, at the end of each story, the ending is always the same:

"Oy! He (or she) suffered so much! May he (or she) rest in peace!"

This brings me to the story of Schmulie Shmendrick.

Schmulie was lying on his death bed with no more than a day left in this world. Because of this, his beloved daughter came to visit.

"Papa! I am here. I came to see you before it was too late. I want to tell you how much I love you!"

"Thank you, my Shaindel." Schmulie replied.

"Papa. Before you go, is there anything I can do for you? Any last wish and I will make sure to take care of it!"

Schmulie's eyes twinkled.

He replied: "That is so thoughtful and sweet, my Shaindel. So, let me tell you. Your mother and I never saw eye to eye. We fought like a cat and a dog. We were like water and oil. We gave each other enough Tsuris to last ten lifetimes. But the one thing that kept us together was your mother's delicious kugel. I know that when I get to heaven, the first thing I will ask for is this special kugel."

He continued:

"You know, I never really knew if your mother actually loved me. But now, I smell her baking that delicious kugel. Not only is she making this delicious kugel, but I can also tell by the smell that she is using only the most expensive potatoes. She would always make it for me with the cheap potatoes, but used the expensive potatoes only for the most special occasion."

He continued:

"With this smell that I now smell, I can die knowing that your mother actually did love me. So, please my sweet Shaindel, can you go into the kitchen, and bring me a piece of this kugel that your mother has so lovingly made so I can have this taste and die a happy man before I leave this world?"

"Sure, Papa. I will go now." Shaindel replied.

Shaindel, the daughter left and went into the kitchen. Schmulie then heard a big commotion with shouting and tussling as if there was a wrestling match in the other room.

Shaindel returned to her father, but she did not have the piece of kugel.

Schmulie asked his daughter:

"Where is the kugel? Did your mother make the tray of kugel?"

Shaindel replied:

"Momma made three trays of kugel."

Schmulie exclaimed:

"Three trays of the kugel! And, with the expensive potatoes! Oy! So where is my piece of kugel?"

Shaindel replied:

"Momma says she is saving it all for the shiva."

CHAPTER 19

BROKEN RECORD CRANKATSURIS

AS I HAVE MENTIONED EARLIER, for many years, my next-door neighbors were the Barkers. The Barker families were Woody and Maple, and their two kids, Birch and Willow. I previously wrote about the Barkers. They used to be the meanest and stingiest people in town. One of them could always be heard saying "You are barking up the wrong tree." If you asked any of them for a favor, the reply was the same. "You are barking up the wrong tree."

However, one day, they all lost their bark. With no bark left in any of the family members, they ultimately were referred to Dr. Sylvia Burt, who happened to be a Barking up the Right Tree specialist. After seeing and working with Dr. Burt, they all became the nicest and most generous family in town. The Barkers' bark all returned.

Recently, I met with Woody Barker, and asked him about this therapy. He was happy to tell me the whole story:

Woody's Story:

Nobody knows this, but we did not go at first to see Dr. Burt. We were sent to see Dr. DESSSiree DISSSaray. This doctor was a doctor whose specialty was to work with people to specifically teach them how not to sweat the small stuff.

We all go to see this Doctor DISSSaray, and I bring up an example of one of our family conflicts. I explained how Birch never cleans his room. I would tell him to clean up, and he snaps back, "You are barking up the wrong tree."

You know what Dr. DISSSaray's advice was? Can you believe it? She tells me, "Let Birch's room be in complete disarray. It is okay if Birch leaves his room a mess! She instructed me, 'Do not sweat the small stuff.'"

I gave the doctor a whole speech when I came back for the second session:

"Doctor, I have lots of problems with your treatment. We all went home, and the first thing I did was check in my garage. I keep all the small stuff in there. None of my small stuff was sweating. I checked the big stuff I keep. None of the big stuff was sweating either. Even if my small stuff did sweat, do you know what happens when you start piling up all the small stuff? You get one huge pile of the big stuff.

"The other thing is that when I get really annoyed at things, I go to work out at the gym. Then, I go to the steam room. Know what happens? I sweat like a pig. I get a good schvitz. After the good schvitz, I actually feel much better. I like to sweat. Correction. I love to sweat. This therapy that does not believe in the pores of the skin opening up for a good schvitz does not work for me.

"Last thing. The other day, we all went to our favorite Chinese restaurant. For dessert, they gave us each a fortune cookie. Do you know what the fortune said? I will tell you. It said, 'Do Not Sweat the Small Stuff.'

"So, we paid you $300 to tell us the exact same thing that we got in a five-cent fortune cookie!"

After this DISSSaray fiasco, we finally ended up with Dr. Burt. Dr. Burt pointed out that we should not focus on the failure to perform a task like cleaning a room. We get frustrated by that. Rather, we should focus on each of the Barker family members to work on fixing all their broken records.

Each of us would get a chance to repeat our broken records. We had to say it over and over again. My broken record was "Clean your room. Clean your room. Clean your room." The family response was to say "Broken record. Broken record. Broken record."

Dr. Burt then focused each of us to come up with ways to fix each other's broken record. If one family member succeeds in fixing another family member's broken record, they get a reward.

Of course, it did not go well when we began the therapy. The first thing we all tried to do was to tape up each other's mouths. Ultimately, we all ran out of tape, and after weeks of work, we started fixing each other's broken records, and then, all of our bark came back!

Believe it or not, Birch fixed my broken record by cleaning up his room! Once he fixed my broken record, I fixed his broken record.

What was that I asked?

"A drum kit, and some drumming lessons!"

My eyes rolled.

"Ok. So, it is not perfect," he said.

This happens to be an important part of our CrankaTsuris practice. We feel that we are not heard. It leads to a CrankaTsuris frustration, and the only thing we know how to do is repeat what was not heard. It is still not heard, or it is heard with resentment. This creates more CrankaTsuris. The CrankaTsuris broken record.

However, if we look at each other's CrankaTsuris as the broken record, we can start to figure out how to fix that broken record. When everybody works to fix the broken record, everybody gets rewarded.

And, that thing about not sweating the small stuff? Because all of the small stuff piled up can become big stuff, with the CrankaTsuris Method, everything gets treated as the "big stuff."

The CrankaTsuris Method is about fixing all of those broken records, big and small!

CHAPTER 20

CRANKATSURIS MOBSTER

THIS IS A STORY ABOUT BIG TONY. Big Tony was the Big Boss of the Big Family. Big Tony also had a big temper. One day, his cousin Vinnie came to talk to Big Tony, and apparently rubbed Big Tony the wrong way. Big Tony had this bad habit that if someone rubbed him the wrong way, chances were that the only thing that this person would end up rubbing would be maybe a rock at the bottom of the Hudson River.

Everybody in the Big Family put up with Big Tony being sensitive to the way he was rubbed because let's face it, he was the Big Boss. Being the Big Boss comes with certain…let's call them CrankaTsuris privileges. However, everybody loved Cousin Vinnie, and when he disappeared, it upset many people in the Big Family.

Big Tony tried to explain himself:

"I am truly sorry about our Cousin Vinnie. I loved him as much as anyone else. I always remember how he got my nephews Johnny and Marco off that murder rap down in Alabama back in the '90s. But, Cousin Vinnie came to me and he was barking up the wrong tree. You bark up the wrong tree, and that shows disrespect. My job is to take care of anyone who barks up the wrong tree. Even Cousin Vinnie."

The Big Family members confronted Big Tony. Big Tony's two uncles, Abbot and Costello, were sent as family representatives to speak with Big Tony:

Abbot: Big Tony, I understand the disrespect, but Cousin Vinnie was just asking you to pass the clam sauce for his pasta. He did not say you had the clams. Well, you did have the clams with the sauce, and that is why he asked you for it.

Costello: Yeah. What he said.

Abbot: I know about this good shrink. She comes highly recommended. Dr. Sylvia Burt. She is a Certified Barking up the Right Tree specialist.

Costello: Yeah. What he said.

Big Tony: Do you think this shrink can help me. Maybe, I am getting a bit sensitive. I feel bad about my Cousin Vinnie. I should let you know that the clams were particularly delicious that night. Muy delichioso!

Abbot: She is the best there is. And yes. The clams in that restaurant are the best! Not a bad clam in the bunch! Ever!

Big Tony went to see Dr. Burt. She got Big Tony to listen better to understand when people were barking up the right tree. However,

Big Tony got too good at letting people bark up his tree, and word started to get out on street to other families. Apparently, it was not good business for the Big Family to let everyone see the Big Boss and have the Big Boss be the right tree for every bark.

The Big Family members became concerned and sent Big Tony's two brothers, Cheech and Chong. These were just their nicknames. Not their real names. Because of a large drug sting involving another family, they were given these names and they are currently in a witness protection program. They were going to have a sit down and talk with Big Tony.

Cheech: Big Tony. We are here to speak with you about a serious matter.

Chong: You are cool with that. Right?

Big Tony: You are barking up the right tree! See. The therapy worked. I do not get upset about anything anymore. What do you get for me today?

Cheech: See. It's like this. You are the Big Boss. Word has gotten out that you have gotten soft, and I think it has something to do with the bark up the right tree thing you have got going here.

Chong: You are cool with that. Right?

Cheech: What Chong means to say is that it has hurt the family business. It is definitely not at all cool. Uncool as can be. Everything is out of whack. The family business is in complete disarray.

Big Tony: So, what are you telling me? Wrong tree. Right tree. What freakin' tree do you want me to be?

Cheech: We thought about this. It is not about trees. We have big stuff that you have to take care of and the small stuff…that is for everyone else.

Chong: We just do not want you to sweat the small stuff. You are cool with that. Right?

Cheech: Yeah. This is the thing. A friend of mine, this guy Woody Barker, told me about this therapist Dr. DESSSiree DISSSaray. She is the best there is in helping patients to learn how not to sweat the small stuff. But she also specializes in helping people sweat the big stuff.

Big Tony went to Dr. DISSSaray. Dr. DISSSaray helped Big Tony to figure out what the small stuff was, and accept that the other family members would take care of the small stuff. But, with the big stuff, Dr. DISSSaray told Big Tony all about the origins of humans, and how they evolved from the TyrantoCrankaTsuris. She got Big Tony to work on his own CrankaTsuris. She got Big Tony to know how and when to release the CrankaTsuris for maximum effect.

Big Tony perfected his CrankaTsuris. He never used it on his own Big Family. But, all the other families in town became terrified of Big Tony's CrankaTsuris. So much so that Big Tony was now known as the Biggest Boss in town!

The Big Family lived happily ever after.

CHAPTER 21

CRANKATSURIS TRAFFIC TIPS

ONE SITUATION THAT GETS PEOPLE ALL WORKED UP and filled with CrankaTsuris are those times when you get stuck in traffic. You are trapped and you have nowhere to go. You need to get somewhere really badly. It is the one time that you could not afford to get stuck in traffic. You know it is bad when you even start to hope to see some terrible traffic accident that caused the terrible traffic jam.

You think to yourself, *It better be something really bad that caused me to sit here for two hours!*

Everyone has had the experience of sitting in a long traffic jam, and you finally get to the point where the traffic begins to move. You then can see the big nothing that delayed your trip for an hour.

The most common "big nothing" is a car pulled over on the other side of the highway by a police car. It did not look very interesting when you passed it, but for everyone else, a car pulled over by the police car apparently was the most exciting event of the week. Apparently, they all had to stop to watch. Maybe, there was one person who even got out of the car and took pictures.

In total disbelief, you start to scream, "I was sitting in traffic for this? I just cannot %&#@ believe it!"

Since Traffic CrankaTsuris is a common form of the CrankaTsuris, here are three tips to follow that will allow you to manage your Traffic CrankaTsuris with ease.

The most important tip is that if you anticipate traffic, make sure you do not drink lots of liquids beforehand. You do not want to be sitting in traffic and then you are stuck and have to pee really badly.

The reason is this. Do you know what the only cure for "Have to Pee Really Badly CrankaTsuris" is? It is called "peeing." And relieving Have to Pee Really Badly CrankaTsuris is the one of two situations that every human on the planet, whether they believe in God or not, will say the same thing. Oh. Thank God!!"

The second most important tip is that if you anticipate traffic is to make sure you do not load your car with little screaming children before you go out. You do not want to be stuck in traffic with screaming kids.

This is the second situation that you finally get home exhausted, and when the kids finally fall asleep, you again exhale, and say "Oh, thank God."

The first two tips lead to the third tip because if you followed Tip One and Tip Two, you could now say the following thing when you get stuck in traffic:

"At least I do not have to pee, and also, at least I do not have screaming kids in the car." Just sit back and enjoy!

Even Traffic CrankaTsuris has a cure!

CHAPTER 22

CRANKATSURIS DAYDREAMS

I HAD A FRIEND WHO STARTED SEEING A THERAPIST. The friend told me that one of the first things that the therapist asked my friend to do was to start writing down all the dreams he had the night before.

I understand that this is something that many therapists ask their patients to do. While I am not against this particular request, I do find it to be a request that is somewhat dishonest. The therapist is not asking the patient to write down dreams. The therapist is asking the patient to write down the nightmares.

Dreams are the stories in your head that you do not want to wake up from. If a therapist asked me to only write down my dreams, I would respond that the dreams are not the problem. It is the waking up part from those dreams that is creating an issue. "That is why I am here to see you. It is about helping me when I am actually awake!"

The other problem I have with writing down all your nightmares is that there isn't anyone to tell you to write down all your daydreams. In fact, it is usually the exact opposite. Try spending a good part of your daydreaming and someone will tell you to stop your daydreaming. "Daydreaming" is apparently seen as a waste of time.

The daydream is in fact a very healthy expression of a CrankaTsuris. Imagine that you are sitting in a class listening to a lecture on how to watch paint dry. I guarantee that if you start to daydream during that lecture, it will not be about how to watch paint stay wet. The daydream will tap into your desires, your hopes, and most importantly, your creativity. The person who stayed alert, and now understands all the facets of how to watch paint dry, will likely be more prone to a greater CrankaTsuris than the person who tapped into their creative juices during a daydream. Albert Einstein may have been a poor student, but he also had the reputation of being a great daydreamer.

We learned about the power and value of daydreaming as children through the story of "The Three Little Pigs." This is not the story that you may have heard as a child, but it is the story that should be told.

Once upon a time, there were three little pigs. Their names were Inky, Pinky, and Stinky. They were very excited because they were about to leave home and go to University. In their first year, they all stayed in the student dormitories that were made out of straw. However, as they approached their second year, they had to decide whether to move off campus into their own homes.

Many pigs decided to move off campus because they heard of a Big Bad Wolf who was heading to town, and could be a danger to the pigs. Some pigs said that the dormitories made out of straw may not be too safe if a wolf came to town, and they needed to live in a home that was a bit safer. Other pigs scoffed at the idea because the word was that the Big Bad Wolf only preyed on old grandmother types, and would not be interested in a porky pig.

All the pig students went to the final lecture of the year. It was an important lecture for all the pigs. The title of the lecture was "Pigs Get Fat. Hogs Get Slaughtered."

Inky was very impressed with the lecture. Inky said to himself that he was a pig, and not a hog. Therefore, he did not have to worry about any silly Big Bad Wolf.

Inky decided to stay in the straw dorm, and one night, the Big Bad Wolf came knocking on the door. When the Big Bad Wolf demanded to let him in, Inky replied that he would not. He would not open the door by the hair of his chinny-chin-chin. The Big Bad Wolf said that is okay. "Do not use your chinny-chin-chin. Open the door with one of your hands. Of course, I could, if you want, just blow the whole house down."

Inky thought to himself that this wolf is rather smart, and besides, why should I worry? I am a pig, and not a hog. The hogs live on the other side of town. The Big Bad Wolf probably ate a few of those hogs and is not very hungry anyway. And I certainly do not want the Big Bad Wolf to blow the house down!

Inky opened the door and was immediately devoured by the Big Bad Wolf.

Pinky loved his brother Inky, and was very traumatized by what happened. He started to have nightmares, and because of these nightmares, he went to see a therapist. The therapist asked Pinky about these nightmares. Pinky told him the following:

"I have this dream that, because of what happened to Inky, I built a house made up of sticks. The sticks were thin, but they were strong. The Big Bad Wolf comes, and threatens to blow my house down, and just at that moment, I wake up in a cold pig sweat."

The therapist told Pinky:

"When you have this dream, write it down immediately. If you have this dream three times, it is a sign that this dream is telling you what to do. You must then go out and find the best sticks, and build a house made out of those sticks. When the Big Bad Wolf comes, just let him try to blow the house down. Besides, the word out there is that he is a chain smoker, and his breath is not all that it is cracked up to be."

Pinky, in fact, had the same dream three times, and following the therapist's instructions, built the finest house in town made out of sticks. When he was finally done building his new home, the Big Bad Wolf paid a visit. When the Big Bad Wolf threatened to blow Pinky's house down, Pinky just laughed.

The therapist was right. The Big Bad Wolf could not blow the house down. However, he saw a loose stick in the bottom of one of the walls. The Big Bad Wolf pulled the stick out and the house of sticks collapsed on top of Pinky. The Big Bad Wolf came in, and quickly devoured poor Pinky.

The next day, despite being very sad about Inky and Pinky, Stinky went to class. The title of the lecture was "Putting Lipstick on a Pig."

It seemed like the lecture went on forever. Stinky thought to himself how silly it was to put lipstick on a pig. Stinky loved to spend the day playing in the mud and had no interest in wearing lipstick. Yuck!

Stinky began to daydream about his favorite activity, playing in the mud, and then realized that the mud was the perfect ingredient to use when making bricks. It just hit Stinky that he could make a house out of bricks, and the Big Bad Wolf would not be able to get into his brick fortress.

Stinky went home and built his house of bricks. Sure enough, the Big Bad Wolf came by, and saw the brick house. He did not even bother to knock, but quickly climbed up and then down the chimney. Once he climbed down the chimney, he smelled the stink of Stinky, and tried to climb back up. But the stink was too much for the Big Bad Wolf. He passed out and fell right into a big pot of stew boiling in the fireplace below.

Everybody in town was very impressed with Stinky's house of bricks. Soon, everyone in town made their own house of bricks. After Stinky lived a long life, the town honored Stinky renaming the town "Stinky Town."

George Carlin, in one of his routines, once said that children should spend at least three hours a day "daydreaming." He wasn't that far off. Perhaps, instead of writing down our nightmares, we should begin to write our daydreams. While we may not get a town named after us, we certainly will experience much less CrankaTsuris.

CHAPTER 23

No Good News
CrankaTsuris

DURING DIFFICULT TIMES, like some of us are experiencing now, everyone is starving for some good news. "I need some good news." "I am desperate for good news." "I never get good news." "When will we finally get some good news?"

These same people are quick to point out the bad news. "It is all bad news." "The only thing we hear is bad news." "I cannot watch the bad news anymore." "I am so done with all the bad news."

This combination can lead to "No Good News CrankaTsuris." This person becomes all gloom and doom. "Unless you have something good to tell me, I do not even want to hear what you have to say."

You would almost have to believe that this same person is acting this way because at some point in their lives, they had lots of good news. It was a good news drug. Because they enjoyed the good news drug, they became a good news drug addict, and is now just suffering from good news drug withdrawal. When you try to point out to this person the fact that the news was not so great before, the response is always the same.

"Yes. The news was bad before. But now it is even worse."

The fact of the matter is that these people were never good news drug addicts, and they are not experiencing withdrawal symptoms.

Finally, you try to cheer this gloomy person up with some good news. "I have good news to report! I got a 95 average on my report card. Yay for me! Doesn't that make you happy? Mom ordered Chinese to celebrate. It is your favorite. Doesn't that make you happy?"

The response usually goes like this. "I am very proud of you, but that is not news. I knew that you would do well. I need news that is good. Chinese food. It is good, but not good news. And can I afford the Chinese food? Maybe, that is bad news."

This same person cannot tell you what good news would look like. This same person usually does nothing to try to create the good news through his or her own actions. They sit on their CrankaTsuris throne, waiting for the good news to be presented to them. They are surprised and upset when the good news fails to arrive. When it does arrive, they can turn the good news into bad news.

"Papa! Once we have the vaccine, the pandemic will be over, and we can go back to normal. That is good news."

"No. It is not good news. It will take years till everything is completely back to normal. I have said it before. This country is going down the tubes. I know. Every morning, I look out the window. Do you know what I see? Tubes. I even hear that when ice caps melt, do you know what they see under the melted ice? Tubes. It used to be one tube. Now, we have many tubes."

While we would all like to get good news, I actually have studied history to find moments of good news. Usually, the good news comes immediately after the really bad news. Because everyone was so happy with the good news after such bad news, they made it a holiday. Independence Day, for example, was the victory over the British. Good news, but it came after the bad news. They had to have a war.

I relate to this fact because I know that many of the holidays in the Jewish religion, which I happen to sometimes follow, was established because they had good news after terrible news.

The holiday of Hanukkah celebrates the overcoming of oppression and persecution by the Greeks and Syrians. The story is one that the news everyday was really terrible, and they overcame what was happening. Good news follows bad news, and we have a holiday.

The story of Purim is one when the evil Haman tricked the King to decree that the Jewish people get exterminated. When you get a decree that you will be kaput, that is awful news. Queen Esther tells the King about the evil plot, and everyone is saved. It is time to create another holiday.

Years before all that, we were slaves in Egypt, building pyramids. It is not much fun being slaves and building pyramids. And, you talk about the heat and the sun they had to endure building the pyramids. If the hard labor didn't kill you, the skin cancer would.

Once again, the news was very bad. It was so bad, they did not need to turn on the television to get their dose of bad news. They lived the bad news. And I can tell you, walking through a desert for forty years was no picnic. Once they got to experience some good news, what is the first thing they did? You guessed it. Another holiday.

Even in our own lives, much of the good news came after bad news. A soon to be mother suffers from morning sickness, lots of kicking and labor pains. Once the baby is born, the first thing we do is throw a party. We remember a day of excruciating pain with a funny clown, silly hats, and goody bags. Another holiday.

But, sometimes, our holidays do not last for long. After years of the terrible twos, threes, and teens, the only thing we can think of is when my child will be on his or her own two feet. Of course, the child is leaving the house, and this is good news. A few days of that, and you realize that the house is now childless. It is bad news. The first thing we complain about is how terrible it is that the house will now be empty. Even the child's wedding day, another holiday, can be a day of good news and bad news.

"Ursula, I hear your daughter is getting married! That is such good news!"

"Zelda, at first, it was good news. But I can tell you after meeting the bum, the only thing I can think about is that she can do so much better!"

But similar to our recognized holidays, the good news after bad news should be a cause for celebration. Joey struggled for years in that job, and he finally got a new job, or he was finally recognized, and got a promotion. Debbie suffered through a terrible marriage, and finally got a divorce. Harry had cancer, but he successfully recovered.

With all this, we see the answer to No Good News CrankaTsuris. If it is because it is the bad news that we are experiencing in our own lives, let this be the opportunity to become resilient and overcome the woes you face. When you are done, you get to claim your own personal holiday.

Of course, if it not the bad news that is affecting you directly, but it is only because you have your television stuck on the bad news channel, the only thing left to do is to turn off the television.

It is another holiday. Have you ever gone on a vacation, and you did not have access to all the newspapers, or the cable news networks, and then, you had to comment how good it was to just get away from the news?

It turns out that what they say is really true.

"No news is good news."

The cure for No Good News CrankaTsuris.

CHAPTER 24

KVETCHER IN THE RYE CRANKATSURIS

IT IS NO DOUBT THAT A GOOD MEAL and some good drink can be a certain cure to almost any CrankaTsuris. However, an unfortunate side effect of this cure is that when things go wrong at mealtime, or the food is just plain bad, the result is an even worse CrankaTsuris. This is what I call "Kvetcher in the Rye CrankaTsuris."

I use the term "Kvetcher in the Rye" because of the many years of experience I had with my father after my parents moved to Florida in the late '90s. For the last ten years they were in an Assisted Living facility in Delray Beach. It was supposedly a treat for my father when I went down every month to visit my parents because it was the one time in the month that I took my father for his haircut, and then, we would go to a Jewish Style deli in Boynton Beach called Flakowitz.

My father always ordered the exact same thing every time we were there. It was a corn beef sandwich on rye, and a small glass of Sprite with no ice. I always had to make sure to tell the waiter to make sure the rye bread for my father's sandwich had no seeds. This was because he had dentures, and it is not fun to get these caraway seeds stuck in your dentures. My father always had one special request when he ordered the corn beef sandwich.

He would tell the waiter:

"I want my corn beef juicy."

Now, anybody who has a craving once in a while for a juicy hamburger may understand the request. Unfortunately, for my father, after he got the sandwich, I would then ask him how it was, and he always had the same answer:

"It is not juicy."

We tried Ben's Deli, and it was the same problem. The corn beef was not juicy. Rueben's Deli also had corn beef that simply was not juicy. Despite the lack of juicy corn beef, we always went to Flakowitz with the hope that, one day, my father would get that juicy corn beef.

I can tell you that we had many lunches that I just wanted to ask the waiter, instead of bringing the usual corn beef sandwich, he should just bring us a nice big glass of corn beef juice with a healthy squirt of mustard, and some half sour pickles just to dunk into the glass of corn beef juice.

If you are reading this now, you are thinking to yourself that a glass of corn beef juice with a squirt of mustard is gross and disgusting. You are correct. But I can tell you what is even more disgusting than that.

Of course, they never brought us the rye bread without the caraway seeds. Apparently, when the waiter heard "no seeds," for some reason, he thought to himself "extra seeds." Though my father did his best to eat the dry corn beef sandwich with the rye bread with extra caraway seeds, the seeds ended up inside the dentures. Halfway through lunch, my father would take his dentures, or what I call his "removable teeth," out of his mouth and place them on the table across from where I was sitting.

While anybody who would look at my father without teeth, and mustard stains all over his shirt would undoubtedly think that he was adorable, it could not make up for being forced to stare at the removable teeth on a table that is covered with chewed up corn beef, rye bread, caraway seeds, and mustard.

After that unfortunate experience, we all came down with a bad case of Kvetcher in the Rye CrankaTsuris.

We all get trained at a very early age to enjoy the experience of Kvetcher in the Rye CrankaTsuris. As you should know, babies do not have teeth. Because of this, the baby food companies actually try to come up with enticing food concoctions that would give a glass of corn beef juice a run for its money.

You may not believe this, but you should look it up. It is true. One of the first jars of baby food that people were able to buy in the local grocery store was "Liver Soup."

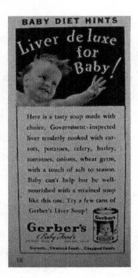

They thought that this was good because not only was it high in nutrients as well as iron, it was also "pleasingly bland," two words that really should never go together in a sentence.

Roommate A: How was that hot date last night?

Roommate B: I hope it went well. She was pleasingly bland!

Roommate A: Do you think she likes you?

Roommate B: She did make a comment that I was bland.

Roommate A: But not pleasingly bland?

Roommate B: She said something about being bland like "liver soup."

Roommate A: Liver soup? Ucch. That is not a good sign.

Liver Soup Baby Food is no longer available for purchase, and for what reason, I cannot tell you. However, you can still go out and purchase chicken with gravy, turkey with gravy, beef with gravy, or ham with gravy. What I am unable to tell you is exactly where one of these meats ends and the gravy begins.

In order to ensure that our child gets the full training and induction in our shared experience of the suffering we endure with Kvetcher in the Rye CrankaTsuris, it is not enough to just shove the gray or brown slime into our child's mouth. We have to convince our baby just how delicious this slime really is. We go into "delicious food baby talk."

"Ooh!! Look what I have! You are in a treat today. Fresh room temperature liver soup! Yummy, yummy, yummy! You are one lucky baby! Open your mouth and let's see you take a nice spoonful! Isn't that good? They say that it is pleasingly bland!"

Of course, we fail miserably, and start to scold the poor little baby who is going through this torture.

"You have to swallow! It is not good manners to have the brown slime just start drooling out of your mouth."

"Honey, can you come over here and help! Baby is not eating. To be honest, I can't blame baby. It looks pretty gross to me!"

"Did you tell baby that the liver soup is pleasingly bland?"

"Yes!"

There are many other food related CrankaTsuris that we all suffer from. For example, many couples suffer from "Return the Food CrankaTsuris." The young couple go out for dinner, and there is one partner who is never happy with the meal and summons the waiter to take the food back. This partner makes the case that they are spending good money for a good meal which gives this person an absolute right to insist on having the food go back to the kitchen and have the chef start from scratch. Usually, it is the man because it is the one time during the week that the poor schmuck can feel like a king!

The other partner is outraged because he or she has to eat their meal while the other person is waiting for a half hour till the new order comes through. Also, this person is annoyed that food is being wasted, and the restaurant will now go out of business just because of the food that had to go to waste. The woman, if it is the woman, thinks to herself, *What a schmuck!*

Both partners stare at each other with a scornful look and smoke coming out of their ears.

I, personally, have suffered over the years from "Ordering the Wrong Food CrankaTsuris." To have this particular malady, you have to go out with a reasonably large group of people. Everyone at the table places an order for something different than the other. The food arrives and everything looks amazing.

Except for whatever I ordered.

The other people at the table will stare at my plate and say, "What is that?"

I shrug and say, "I do not know. I thought I was getting something else and I guessed I ordered the wrong thing."

I have gone to restaurants, and in a desperate attempt not to order the wrong thing, I even ask the waiter what he or she recommends.

The waiter then describes the Chef's Specialty. I am assured that it is delicious and that I could not possibly go wrong. I proceed to order the Chef's Special Dish. However, I am sure the Chef and the Waiter have this conversation in the kitchen.

Chef: Isn't that the guy who orders the wrong thing all the time?

Waiter: Indeed, he is.

Chef: Ok. I will make sure to make it especially wrong, just for him.

Waiter: Very good.

So, as you can see, there are many forms or variants of Kvetcher in the Rye CrankaTsuris. In fact, it is one of the most common forms of CrankaTsuris so it must be effectively dealt with as well. Of course, one solution would be for all of us to go on a strict smoothie diet. However, that probably would not be very practical, and it would not be much fun either.

There are solutions to this problem, of course. The first thing is to realize we are all Kvetchers in the Rye, in one way or the other. That means that if one person becomes a Kvetcher in the Rye, try not to be judgmental. You have had the experience of Kvetcher in the Rye CrankaTsuris yourself. Having empathy is one way to soothe the CrankaTsuris.

The second thing you can do is always remember that you are going out to share each other's company. The company should always be primary, and not the food. This is an important rule unless you are eating by yourself.

The third thing you can do is always have the habit of sharing each other's meal. This is particularly useful if one partner returns an order. If that happens, have the waiter split the first order in two, and then the couple could reorder the second dish together. That means that if you are returning that overcooked steak, but your partner does not eat steak, you will have to find a second dish you both enjoy. You then get to split the second entree.

When people share the food, it becomes a shared experience. It is a shared experience of not only the good, but the bad as well. Hopefully, nobody will get food poisoning from trying this out.

The fourth and most important thing you can do is to keep your teeth in your mouth. Just remember. Once you start taking the teeth out, there is no cure for Kvetcher in the Rye CrankaTsuris.

CHAPTER 25

TOUGH GOING
CRANKATSURIS

THEY ALWAYS TELL YOU THE SAME THING. "When the going gets tough, the tough get going."

Now, I have a real problem with this statement. When the going gets tough, apparently the tough never stick around. Therefore, the tough never get any experience whatsoever in dealing with the tough going. If these tough folks have the reputation of being so tough, how did they even get this reputation if they have no experience dealing with any of these tough situations? I happen to think that if you really want to have this "tough" reputation, you need to stick around for at least seventy-five percent of the time. You cannot always get going whenever the going gets tough.

If you stick around when the going gets tough, one of the side effects is that you may experience some crankiness, and even let out a CrankaTsuris along the way. This should not be seen as something to necessarily avoid, but rather, this experience is part of starting to embrace our crankiness, and even part of our development in being able to be effectively cranky.

Let me share a story that will show you exactly what I mean by all of this.

Once upon a time, there were two brothers. One brother was called "Timid Timmy," and the other brother was called "Tommy Tough Nuts." Timmy was called timid because he always acted in a timid sort of way. Tommy was known as "Tough Nuts" because he always liked to say:

"When the going gets tough, the tough get going. It would be nuts to stick around!"

Their mom would come yell into their bedrooms:

"Timmy!! Tommy! Please clean up your rooms right now!"

Timmy was feeling timid, and a little cranky. He decided that while he did not like the feeling of being cranky, it would be better not to make mom angry, so he decided to clean up his room.

Tommy saw the time, and remembered that he was supposed to meet his friends outside. He told his mom:

"Mom. I promised my friends that I would meet them at the candy shop so I have to get going. And when the going gets tough, the tough get going. It would be nuts to stick around!"

Whenever it was time to study for their exams, Timmy was feeling a bit timid. He wanted to do well and was afraid that he was not fully prepared. He decided that rather than go outside and play, he would stay home and study. Timmy was not happy about staying home. He would much rather go out and play with his other friends. Timmy was feeling quite cranky about this.

Timmy asked his brother Tommy if he was staying home to study. Tommy saw the time and remembered that he was supposed to meet his friends outside. Tommy looked at Timmy and laughed. He replied:

"That is so boring, and a waste of time. As I always say, when the going gets tough, the tough get going. It would be nuts to stick around. Who needs to learn math anyway when we have computers to give us the answers."

Both Timmy and Tommy had piano lessons. Timmy always felt timid and made sure he would always practice and be ready for the next lesson. This made Timmy very cranky at times. Piano practice was always very boring. However, no matter how cranky it made him, he kept practicing.

Tommy never spent much time practicing. It was too boring. When it was time to practice, Tommy saw the time, and remembered that he was supposed to meet his friends outside.

When Tommy was asked about whether he was staying home to practice, he said to Timmy:

"That is so boring. As I always say, when the going gets tough, the tough get going. Our piano teacher doesn't even care if I play well or not. It would be nuts to stick around!"

Years later, Timmy developed many skills. He was a successful concert pianist, and later went to medical school and ultimately became a well-known surgeon. Whenever there was a tough operation, Timmy was the one everyone wanted. Timmy was even called "Timmy, One Tough Operator."

Because poor Tommy never stuck around for anything, Tommy was never good at anything. He never accomplished much, and everyone said that he was rather timid. Not only did Tommy have a reputation for being timid, some people said that he also was a little bit nuts at times. He definitely had to experience a lot of CrankaTsuris.

Use this story to remind you what Effective Crankiness is all about. It is about growth, and opportunity. It is about taking on what may appear to be difficult, and with some hard work, becoming a master at a craft. When you think about your crankiness with the possibility of what you can achieve, it puts crankiness in a whole new positive light.

And if you always got going when the going got tough, perhaps that is what leads to all that ineffective crankiness.

It is never truer than when you confront "Tough Going CrankaTsuris."

CHAPTER 26

PET PEEVES
CRANKATSURIS

THERE IS ONE THING THAT EVERYONE HAS IN COMMON. We all have had pets in our lives. I am not necessarily talking about a pet dog, or a cat, a goldfish, or even a pet rattlesnake. I am talking about our beloved pet peeves. Some people have so many pet peeves, you could start to imagine that they must be spending most of their time taking care of animals at the local zoo.

Then, there are people in a relationship when one person has so many pet peeves that the other person, just so this person does not have to listen to all the pet peeves, start to take up many pet projects. Of course, the pet projects become a major pet peeve for the other partner. The partner with the pet projects now has a pet peeve that the other person is always complaining about the pet projects.

Oy.

When my parents got older, I suggested that, perhaps, my brother and I can buy them a pet. Their response was always the same:

"We are too old to have any pets."

I can now finally understand.

The big question is why we even call these peeves we have "pets." It certainly would make a whole lot more sense if we call our personal peeves "pest peeves." If I am thinking about a name for a pet, I may name my pet "Fluffy" or "Whiskers." Nobody would consider "Peeve" as a proper name for their pet.

Growing up in the Bronx in the 1970s, during the day, the men would typically be at work. The women would gather together downstairs, and sit on benches in the back, sharing their pet peeves.

Woman 1: I can't take it anymore. I have to constantly nag my husband to chew his food. Sometimes, I burn his steak on purpose just to make it a bit drier and tougher, and somehow, he is still able to inhale it. He tells me that he is practicing for when he gets old and loses all his teeth. He proudly says that he will be the only person in the nursing home who can still eat solid food.

Woman 2: My husband chews, and I can't take it anymore. My husband has perfected at least a dozen animal sounds between his chewing, and then, there is the snoring. Oy. Forget it! I would be happy if he could just stick with one animal. One day, it is a donkey with the "Eeeh Orrrr, Eeeh Orrrr" and the next day, it will be a lamb or a goat. "Baah, baaah." And the pig noise he makes! I never even knew pigs can make that kind of noise. Did I tell you that the noises come out of everybody opening? I just can't take it anymore!

Woman 3. Do I have a story! I got tired of cleaning out the stains in his underwear. I even started to buy him black underwear. Only my husband can get stains in black underwear that does not come out. Finally, I couldn't take it anymore. So, I convinced him to wear diapers.

Woman 1: You got him to wear diapers? How? I have the same problem with my husband, and I can't take it anymore!

Woman 2: I would use bleach, and my husband refused to wear them. He didn't like the smell of the bleach, or the bleach blotches on his underwear. I like to hear how, too! I can't take it anymore!

Woman 3: Well first, he agreed to it because that meant that he would not have to listen to my pet peeve complaining about his underwear. He then decided that he would take on a pet project, and he spends the whole weekend painting his diapers. He calls it "Diaper Art." He has a collection that he wants to display at the Museum of Modern Art.

Woman 1: At least, your husband has found himself an artistic outlet.

Woman 2: You should invite us over to see this art exhibit before it goes public!

Woman 3: You do not understand. My husband thinks that he has also created this new great product. "Diapers for Grownups." Do you want to know what he calls them?

Woman 1 and Woman 2 nodded their heads as they were both very curious.

Woman 3: "Gripers." Apparently, my husband thinks that he has a lot to gripe about. I just can't take it anymore.

Woman 1 and Woman 2: Oy.

Later in life, my next-door neighbors were the Barker family. If you have been reading this book, you should already know all about the

Barkers. The Barkers were Woody and Maple, and their two kids, Bossy Birch and Whiny Willow. If anybody would ever ask them for a favor, they all had one singular response.

"You are barking up the wrong tree."

They actually had a pet dog. He was a mangy and ugly looking sort of dog, and the Barkers gave their pet dog the name of Peeve. He was actually so mangy looking that he looked like a dog that would be named "Peeve."

The problem was that none of the Barkers took care of their pet Peeve. Whiny Willow was always too busy with her pet project which was her beloved dollhouse. Bossy Birch was always too busy with his pet project which was his beloved train set.

If Woody or Maple would ask either Bossy Birch or Whiny Willow to take Peeve out for a walk, the response was always the same.

"You are barking up the wrong tree."

Because Peeve was constantly ignored by the Barkers, this was Peeve's own pet peeve, and with every day that he was ignored, Peeve's pet peeve got bigger and bigger until one day, he could not take it anymore. So, one night, while Bossy Birch and Whiny Willow were asleep, their pet, Peeve, came in and destroyed both the doll house and the train set. The dolls and the train tracks were all chewed up, and it looked like one big disaster area.

Even worse, that morning when Bossy Birch and Whiny Willow woke up, they, along with the parents, discovered that they all lost their bark. Their pet, Peeve, however, was gleefully barking away, proud of his accomplishment.

The Barkers, of course, went to see Dr. Sylvia Burt, who was a recognized Barking up the Right Tree specialist. Once the Barkers learned how to bark up the right tree, they all got back their bark.

Birch and Willow were no longer bossy or whiny, and when they came home, they decided to give their pet Peeve a nice shampoo bath. After the bath, they brushed Peeve's fur, and they noticed that Peeve was not mangy at all. In fact, it turned out that he was quite fluffy.

That night, Birch and Willow decided to give their pet Peeve a new name: "Fluffy."

Since we all have our "pet peeves," it can easily be understood that these pet peeves can become a "Pet Peeves CrankaTsuris." Then, when one person lets out a Pet Peeves CrankaTsuris, the partner receiving this particular CrankaTsuris reminds Partner One of their own Pet Peeves CrankaTsuris. This CrankaTsuris tends to be a bit louder because the belief of any person letting out a Pet Peeves CrankaTsuris is that they happen to have the superior pet peeve.

This then spirals into a showdown at the Pet Peeves CrankaTsuris Olympics. Each partner wants to win the Pet Peeves CrankaTsuris gold medal!

Again, this is where the CrankaTsuris Method can be useful. We recognize each other's pet peeve. We can laugh about a few, and agree that others can be quite irritating. We can even decide that one pet peeve is so irritating that it is worthy of being converted into a pet project.

Then, maybe we should give a new meaning to the term "pet peeve," and think about why it isn't called a "pest peeve," If we think about our pets that we love, it does not mean that they do not peeve us sometime. They want a walk when you are feeling exhausted. They had an accident on the rug that you have to now clean up. They went in and destroyed your closet during a thunderstorm. After all that, there is still some unconditional love left.

If we remember all the reasons we love each other, maybe a little pet peeve isn't that bad after all.

CHAPTER 27

CONSTRUCTIVE CRITICISM CRANKATSURIS

WHEN I GREW UP IN THE BRONX, my favorite comedian was Rodney Dangerfield. He was a fellow New Yorker who I could relate to when he said that he got no respect at all. I also loved how he showed how happy he was when he went on stage. "What a crowd! What a crowd!" He then would tell the audience "I am okay now. But, last week, I tell you. I was in bad shape."

I imagine that he got the idea of his "No Respect" routine after many people in his inner circle would criticize young Rodney and they would always start the critical comment by saying "In all due respect."

I find the phrase "in all due respect" to be a rather interesting one because when someone wants to tell you something "in all due respect," it never means that this person finally wants to give you the respect you deserve. In fact, the phrase "in all due respect" actually is used to tell you that you deserve no respect at all.

I picture in my mind that Rodney Dangerfield was one of those door-to-door vacuum cleaner salesman I would see on a sitcom. One of the very funny bits is when the salesman comes in and tells the poor woman trying to clean up the house that he has the solution to all her problems. He then proceeds to invade her home, and sees a plate of spaghetti with tomato sauce. He spills it onto the rug. He opens up the refrigerator and sees a can of beer. He pours it on the rug as well. After five more items gets tossed or poured on to the rug, he attempts to clean it up with his miracle vacuum, and nothing happens.

We are then taken to the next scene when the salesman is tossed out, and his miracle machine gets tossed out with him. Finally, to add insult to injury, the salesman gets a taste of his own medicine as tomato sauce gets sprayed all over him.

At some point, the Big Boss calls Rodney into his office. The conversation goes like this:

Big Boss: Rodney, can you come in here?

Rodney: Yes, Big Boss.

Big Boss: Rodney. Let me tell you something with all due respect.

Rodney starts for a second to daydream. The Big Boss will tell him something with all due respect! He will finally be getting the respect he deserves and so much craves! Perhaps, he will even get a promotion!

Big Boss: I forgot my train of thought. What was I saying?

Rodney: Respect! You were talking about all my due respect.

Big Boss: Yah, yah. Rodney, with all due respect, nobody really likes you around here. We have no idea of what you are doing. So, we are firing you. Pack your bags and leave.

Rodney: I can't believe it. But, what about my due respect?

Big Boss: Okay. You are not very bright either. Now, get out of my sight!

Rodney goes home and tells his wife the bad news. She has a disgusted look on her face, and starts to say, "with all due respect." Rodney thinks for a second that his wife will give him the support he needs. She is not going to kick a man when he is down, Rodney reasons to himself.

Wife: Rodney, with all due respect, I have to say my parents were right. I married a loser! Why don't you see your son upstairs? He said he needs to ask you something.

Rodney thinks to himself that at least his son needs him. He should be appreciative that, at least, he has that.

Rodney: Son, I am so happy to see you. Your mother said you wanted to ask me something.

Son: Yes, Dad. Can I borrow $500?

Rodney: $500!! I just got fired from my job! I do not have that kind of money. Anyway, what do you need $500 for?

Son: My class is having "Bring Your Father to School Day." You know. It is when the father comes in and tells the class what amazing job he has. I need the $500 to hire Tommy's dad to come in and pretend he is my father. His dad is the chef of that restaurant that just got great reviews. With all due respect, Dad, you are a loser. It would be embarrassing to have you come in. You understand. Right?

Rodney mutters to himself: "No respect. I get no respect at all."

And the rest was history.

Related to the phrase "with all due respect" is when people that are closest to you want to give you "constructive criticism." If you are lucky, they may ask you for permission to give you some constructive criticism, or they may call it "a little feedback." It is always called "a little feedback" because we all know that nobody wants to get a whole bunch of feedback. We humans are simply not wired to handle a whole bunch of feedback. Just a little feedback is as much as we can handle.

However, all too often, the constructive criticism is constructed together with a CrankaTsuris, and there was no permission to give this CrankaTsuris. The person who receives the "Constructive Criticism CrankaTsuris" responds with his or her own Constructive Criticism CrankaTsuris. The result is that nobody takes in the criticism or feedback which only leads to more CrankaTsuris.

Of course, there are exceptions to this rule if it is coming from your Jewish mother who will only speak Yiddish when it is solely for the purpose of providing you with constructive criticism. I got some sagely Jewish mother advice with sayings like these:

"Don't be a Paskudnyak!"

Now, the word "Paskudnyak" means a nasty or contemptible person. A rascal. A boy who makes mischief. Now, if my mother said to me that I was a nasty or contemptible person I may have been crushed by such a comment. I would never recover. *My mother hates me!* I would think to myself.

However, being called a "Paskudnyak" was something special. It was status. It gave me a sense of pride while at the same time I knew that maybe I should try to be a little bit less of a Paskudnyak.

My mother would also like to instruct me:

"Don't be a Moyshe Groise with tsirissena gatkas!"

This just means "Don't be the great Moses with torn underwear."

I always loved this advice because my mother would only tell me this when my underwear happened to be torn. In other words, I was getting a big compliment. My mother actually was comparing me to the great Moses.

Other than these two exceptions, or if you have developed your own affectionate language for giving constructive criticism or feedback, if the constructive criticism is just Constructive Criticism CrankaTsuris, it will likely not be very effective or well received. It could very well end up as destructive instead of constructive. Both parties involved may very well find themselves stuck in the dog house.

For those who have never been in a dog house, it is not a very pleasant place. It is dark and stuffy. There are no windows. It is cold in the winter. It is hot in the summer. You have cobwebs and spiders all over. Roaches and rats are crawling around. It is a scary place to be. This why even a dog does not like the doghouse, and they end up sleeping with you in your comfy bed.

Because of this problem, it is important for us to know how to avoid Constructive Criticism CrankaTsuris. The first rule is that the criticism or feedback actually has to be constructive. You have to have some reasonable belief that this criticism or feedback will actually be helpful for the other person. It will also be so helpful that the other person will want to hear it.

The best example of this is the batting coach working with a hitter. The hitter has been popping up because his swing has been too "uppercut," and this causes all of those pop ups. The coach then talks about the uppercut swing, and helps the hitter to flatten it out a bit. The results are line drive hits into the gaps in the outfield. The hitter then makes the All-Star Team.

The second rule is to think about giving the criticism as if you are in a negotiation. I teach people how to negotiate, and the big mistake people make in negotiation is that they are solely focused on getting their best deal. I have to explain to people that you have to assume that the opposing side will not necessarily care about your best deal. In fact, they don't.

I would love to go to a mediation, which is where I typically end up negotiating, and when I arrive, the opposing and adverse attorney sees me, and right away says:

"Steve! So good to see you! I do not want my client to hear this, but you know how good I made you look last time. This time, I will make you look like an absolute genius."

This will never happen. The other side's objective is never to give me my best deal. As I have said, they don't really care about my best deal. Yes. I know. It is very sad. However, I always tell people that I can never expect to make a deal because I am making arguments why it is my best deal. I have to make arguments why it is the other side's best deal. My expectation is that they will do the same. If we are focused on each other's best deal instead of our own, do you know what ends up happening? We both end up getting our best deal.

The third rule is that you have to understand that the reason you want to give the constructive criticism or feedback is that whatever the other person is doing, it is causing you to have a CrankaTsuris. That is why it is too often that we attach the constructive criticism to the actual CrankaTsuris we are experiencing. We have to separate the CrankaTsuris from the constructive criticism, and it is okay to let the other person know that whatever is happening is causing a CrankaTsuris to form inside you, but you will be sure to let the CrankaTsuris subside before giving the constructive criticism or feedback.

The fourth rule is that it has to be presented with all due respect. This means that you have to provide some due respect. If it is done respectfully, it will more likely be heard.

The fifth rule is that if the first four rules do not work, you can just give the constructive criticism that my loving mother gave me.

"Don't be a Paskudnyak!"

Of course, if you follow all of these rules, then you too can happily say:

"What a crowd! What a crowd! I am okay now, but let me tell you. Last week I was in bad shape."

With all due respect, this is the cure for Constructive Criticism CrankaTsuris.

CHAPTER 28

Don't Want Your Opinion CrankaTsuris

Don't Want Your Opinion CrankaTsuris is a particularly interesting CrankaTsuris to explore because it can lead to other forms of CrankaTsuris such as Constructive Criticism CrankaTsuris, Get Off My Back CrankaTsuris, Getting on My Nerves CrankaTsuris, or Drive Me Crazy CrankaTsuris. Just imagine if you came down with all four CrankaTsurises at the exact same time! Things can get pretty ugly pretty quickly.

It starts with someone, usually your partner (or your boss, perhaps), wanting to give you an opinion that also has a request tied in with it. Your partner wants to tell you to do something, along with the opinion as to exactly how you should do it. The reason that your partner is so eager to give you an opinion on how to complete the task is because your partner already has had a lifetime of experience of you incorrectly and incompetently completing this simple task.

You make it clear that you do not want their opinion because you know that it means that you have to do something, and also to be reminded of all the times you kind of screwed up. The fact that you do not want this person's opinion does not diminish this person's desire to give you an opinion because this person wants you to do something, and also, to do the thing their particular way.

After a while, when it becomes abundantly clear that you will be getting the opinion, regardless of whether you want this opinion or not, you relent and agree to accept this person's opinion, and understand that you will have a job to do. You hear the opinion, or at least you think you heard the opinion. Now that you heard the opinion, you disagree with the opinion.

The primary reason that you disagree with the opinion is because it requires you to do the something that you do not want to do, or if it is something that you were going to do, it is not the way you were going to do it. You have no memory whatsoever of previously doing this task incorrectly. It may have been a traumatic event that you conveniently deleted from your memory bank. However, you see that it is very important for this other person that you complete the task that you did not want to do, so you then reluctantly agree to do what this other person asked you to do.

Probably because you did not want the opinion in the first place, and did not want to do what was requested in the second place, and if you were ever willing to do what was requested, it was not the way you would even do it in the third place, you end up doing the thing that was requested in the exact opposite way it was suggested that you do what had been asked.

This, you believe, should satisfy the person who offered the opinion which became a request that you had, as you firmly believe, generously agreed to do. You had agreed to do this task because you felt that you were about to come down with Get Off My Back CrankaTsuris, and you wanted this person to get off your back without the CrankaTsuris.

However, because you completed the task in a way that was diametrically opposed to the way the other person requested that you do the task, this person lets you know very quickly, and you then come down with the exact thing you were avoiding: a bad case of "Get Off My Back CrankaTsuris." You do not even realize that you completed the task in a way that was not asked. You believe that you followed the directions exactly as requested.

This then adds to the CrankaTsuris. You have now come down with a case of "Drive Me Crazy CrankaTsuris." It drives you crazy when somebody asks you to do something that you did not want to do in the first place, and instead of getting a thank you for going out of your way to do what was asked, you get a very angry person who also comes down with both Drive Me Crazy CrankaTsuris, and I Can't Understand How CrankaTsuris:

> "I tell this bum to do one simple thing that no human could possibly botch up, and amazingly, he figures out a way to botch it up. I can't understand how! It drives me crazy when I make a request, this person tells me that they are going to do it, and then they proceed to do the exact opposite."

The bum's partner now also has Drive Me Crazy CrankaTsuris.

Both participants in this terrible interaction now come down with Getting on My Nerves CrankaTsuris. They are also suffering from a case of Constructive Criticism CrankaTsuris. This particular combination is a bad and dangerous case of this particular CrankaTsuris, because not only have they gotten on each other's nerves and not only have they both rubbed each other the wrong way, they have now gotten underneath each other's skin. This is the trifecta of Getting on My Nerves CrankaTsuris.

One person in this dispute charges the other person that not only did this person not hear what was said in this particular instance. The charge is expanded to "You never ever listen to me. You do not even know how to pay attention," further adding to the Constructive Criticism CrankaTsuris.

The other person, in response, charges back that everything that was said was in fact heard, but now, with this complaint, the response is that "I will never, ever listen to you again!"

Hearing this, the person who initiated the charge, responds by saying: "Do you want my opinion?"

The second person, who just a second ago said "I will never ever listen to you ever again" feels guilty about this threat and what that actually would mean in the relationship, responds, "Ok. What is your opinion?"

The first person responds, "We should go see a therapist."

The second person does not want to see a therapist, and again goes back to this belief that everything was heard, and if it was not heard, certainly the hearing will vastly improve since the belief is that even improved hearing is better than seeing a therapist. However, the second person may be smart enough to know that they would not be able to convince the first person about improved listening skills so the second person agrees to go to see the therapist.

The couple goes to the therapist who listens to their communication problem. The therapist then gives them an opinion. Both partners are actually quite happy with the opinion because they each conformed the opinion to what they wanted to hear. On the way home, they discovered this disconnect, and it reverts back to each suffering from Drive Me Crazy CrankaTsuris.

This gets me to an old Buddhist story about the four blind men and an elephant. It is a story of a group of blind men who have never come across an elephant before and who learn and imagine what the elephant is like by touching it. None of them were aware of its shape and form.

Out of curiosity, they said: "We must inspect and know it by touch, of which we are capable." So they sought it out, and when they found it, they groped about it. The first person, whose hand landed on the trunk said, "This being is like a thick snake." For the second, whose hand reached its ear, it seemed like a kind of fan. As for the third, whose hand was upon its leg, he said, "The elephant is a pillar, like a tree-trunk." The blind man who placed his hand upon its side said the elephant "is a wall." Another who felt its tail, described it as a rope. The last felt its tusk, stating the elephant is that which is hard, smooth, and like a spear. Each blind man felt a different part of the elephant's body, but only a single part, such as the side or the tusk.

Of course, each of the men described the elephant based on their limited experience and their descriptions of the elephant are different from each other. They come to suspect that the other person is dishonest and they come to blows. The moral of the parable is that humans have a tendency to claim absolute truth based on their limited, subjective experience as they ignore other people's limited, subjective experiences which may be equally true.

I refer to this parable because sometimes, it really comes down to really examining the elephant in the room. There are things that we want to hear. There are things that we may be able to hear. There are the things that we may need to hear. Each may be very different from each other.

The things that we want to hear is the most limited. It starts with the story that has already formed in our head. As an attorney, I am used to seeing people litigate disputes because that is what litigation is about. However, since I am in the world of litigation, once I step outside of that bubble, I get to witness regular people do that every day. I can succumb to that temptation at times well. It is, unfortunately, a human instinct we all have. People sometimes want to win or be in the right. Of course, these people are not professionals, and it often gets ugly.

At this point, we can try to drop the story. If we drop the story, the litigation that we all do can stop as well. Then, we need to find a replacement. There is one that is always available, and it is called generosity. Sometimes, we can feel generous, and sometimes, not so much. That is okay too. As long as we are being honest. Honesty too is respected. However, we can let the other person know when we can feel generous. When we can clearly express the fact that we are feeling generous, we are more open. Then, the practice of generosity can be met with generosity in return.

As a negotiator, this generosity is called giving the other side the experience of being heard. When you give someone that experience, you can get that generosity back in return. Soon, the Don't Want Your Opinion CrankaTsuris can be replaced with "I am very interested in your opinion."

And just like that, maybe we are ready to examine the entire elephant in the room.

CHAPTER 29

COWS COME HOME CRANKATSURIS

COWS COME HOME CRANKATSURIS typically occurs in a "couples" setting. One partner starts to argue with the other, but the other is not listening. In fact, the other responds with arguments of his or her own. Both sides want desperately to win the argument, and when they realize that they are not being heard, each person raises their voice louder and louder until it turns into a fully-fledged Cows Come Home CrankaTsuris.

One partner screams, "You are mad at me? I am the one who should be mad at you!!" This, by the way, does not magically end the madness. Both partners can argue all they want, and it would not make any difference. They can argue forever until the "cows come home." This is a big problem because neither partner never even owned a cow.

As an attorney, I teach negotiation skills to other attorneys. One of the first things I tell attorneys is that in a negotiation, arguments will take away your power. Attorneys, at first, find this to be quite distressing because the big reason that they went to law school in the first place was because they love to argue. If they are not allowed to argue, they fear that they will just wither away and die.

However, to make my point, the conversation goes something like this:

Me: Tell me your negotiation strategy.

Young Lawyer: I plan to argue Point A.

Me: Does your opposing counsel know about Point A?

Young Lawyer: Yes. That is why they will argue Point B.

Me: Do you believe you will convince your opposing counsel of Point A?

Young Lawyer: Of course not. My opposing counsel has already convinced herself of Point B.

Me: Will your opposing counsel then convince you of Point B?

Young Lawyer: Of course not. I have convinced myself that Point A is the correct position.

Me: Do either of you own any cows?

Young Lawyer: Of course not. Why do you ask?

Me: Because you can both argue till the cows come home.

The point here is that nobody will give you credit for the argument they already knew you were going to make. However, this does not mean that you give up making arguments. Rather, you need to be mindful as to how you will present your argument. The instruction for lawyers is to present your position in the most factual way possible, and then draw upon those facts to reach the most logical conclusion. I should not have to argue that the world is round. It just happens to be round.

You also will need to be able to show that you heard the other side. "I understand that it is your position that the Earth is flat. I can understand that. You look outside and see flat. However, would you be interested in seeing pictures of the Earth from outer space?"

People will more likely hear what you have to say if you have shown that you have heard them as well.

Another effective way to deal with Cows Come Home Cranka Tsuris is to always be curious and ask questions. The act of asking questions tells the person that you are with that you are engaged, and you are hearing what they have to say. You also may disagree with what the person has to say, but that disagreement may not be apparent to the other person because the questions you ask may be the questions that the other person had not yet thought of.

Years ago, when I was in law school in Pittsburgh, I went to Saturday morning services. The Rabbi took a liking to me, and always invited me for lunch after services. During lunch, the Rabbi liked to discuss the Torah (Bible) reading from that morning. Sometimes, he would want to discuss the Gemara. The Gemara is a collection of books that house the various texts of rabbis from many generations ago providing analysis and commentary on various aspects of Jewish law or what is called the Mishnah. The Rabbi thought I would appreciate such discussions since I was studying to become a lawyer.

One particular Saturday, we had the discussion about the time that the Jewish people were wandering in the desert, and Moses sent a team of spies to the Land of Israel to learn about the people that were inhabiting the land, and presumably, the people that they would have to possibly fight to take over the land.

Some of the spies came home terrified because they saw that the Land of Israel was inhabited by giants. My question to the Rabbi was first, were these people really giants. The Rabbi took a very literal interpretation of the Bible, and said to me, in a matter of fact manner, that they were indeed giants.

My question was then, if they were in fact, giants, why were they so terrified. How hard could it be to defeat a giant? You take a slingshot and a pebble. In a second, Boom! Down goes the giant!

I reasoned that I would be more terrified if the spies came back and told everyone that the Land of Israel was inhabited by midgets. First, we were continuously told that this is the Land of Milk and Honey. If everyone there were very small people, I would be very scared to start eating and drinking this special milk and honey that everyone was talking about.

Also, if we ended up defeating midgets, my ancestors at the Passover Seder would be telling this story, and one of the four questions would be "Why can't we pick on someone our own size?"

Not only that. We, ourselves, would be midgets asking this question!

Now, if the land was in fact inhabited by giants, I would be very excited to get some of this amazing and magical milk and honey! I would think to myself "This year Jerusalem. Next year, I will be dunking over Michael Jordan!"

The Rabbi knew that I was a joker, and appreciated the humor, but I could see in his eyes that he was starting to think that maybe these people may not have been giants after all. Or maybe they were. Who knows for sure?

My favorite Gemara discussion involved the judges who were present during the time of the First Temple who made a ruling that the fat of the cow's third stomach was kosher. Afterwards, they realized that they made a mistake, and it was in fact not kosher.

It gets even better. These same judges then rule that the second ruling was incorrect, and the fat of the cow's third stomach was in fact kosher. However, months later, these same judges reversed their ruling once again. The fat of the cow's third stomach was indeed not kosher.

This raised the question of whether the people who ate the cow fat and sinned by relying upon the judges' ruling had to bring a sin offering to the temple, or should only the judges be required to bring a sin offering since it was their error in their rulings that caused people to eat the fat in the first place.

The rabbis in the Gemara ruled that the judges had to bring a sin offering. The people would only be required to bring a sin offering if half or more than half of the population ate the fat of the cow's third stomach. Given that this mistake happened twice, you can combine the group of people who ate the fat after the first ruling with the people who ate the fat after the second ruling. You do not have to count a person twice if they ate the fat after both the first and second incorrect ruling.

This, of course, raised many important questions. Of course, I did not ask the most important question. Why are we even discussing something that really cannot be applied in any way today? Many people who would listen to something like this may even want to argue that it is all gibberish. Of course, that argument would lead to Cows Come Home CrankaTsuris and the person who made that argument would never be invited to Saturday lunch again.

My first question was "who were these judges who made so many mistakes?" Couldn't they set up an appellate court or even a Supreme Court to make a final ruling? That would make the mistakes more understandable.

The bigger question involved this 50% threshold. The first question is how they even counted the people who ate the cow fat that the number of people met this high percentage. Did they take down names with each sale? Were they able to scan credit card purchases? The second and more pressing question to me was how likely would it be that half the Jewish population would run out to get the fat of the cow's third stomach once they heard the ruling.

Murray: Shirley! Did you hear the wonderful news? The judges ruled today that the fat of the cow's third stomach is kosher!

Shirley: Murray. What do you need with the fat of the cow's third stomach? The cow has four stomachs. Tell me. The fat from three stomachs is not enough for you? And, you know what the doctor said. You are a heart attack waiting to happen. Your cholesterol level is through the roof. You have to cut back on your fat intake!

Murray: But, before I die, I want to taste the fat of the cow's third stomach!

Shirley: Fine. When you are lying on your deathbed, I will be sure to bring you a piece.

I told the Rabbi that I did not think it was possible to reach 50% on this one. Of course, if the judges ruled that lobster and shellfish became kosher, it would be very easy to count the 50%.

"Breaking News: A caravan of Jews is heading towards the Maine border! The word is that they are all going to a giant lobster and clambake!"

Again, the Rabbi had a good sense of humor, and he appreciated the questions as well. Questions create thought.

You may now be wondering where the phrase "You can argue till the cows come home" even comes from. I happen to have that answer as well.

Again, we come back to our friend, Mr. Schlemiel. Mr. Schlemiel always wanted to own a chicken farm. When he saw Mr. Schmegeggi's "Chicken Farm for Sale" advertisement, Mr. Schlemiel called Mr. Schmegeggi right away and purchased the farm. The only problem was that the farm had no chickens. All of the chickens had crossed the road to get to the other side. The reason that the chickens crossed the road to get to the other side was that the grass was always greener on the other side.

Years went by, and the farm still had no chickens. Mr. Schlemiel would confront Mr. Schmegeggi about this, and Mr. Schmegeggi always assured him. "Soon, you will see. One day, your chickens will come home to roost!"

Mr. Schlemiel felt reassured from this comment. His wife was not. Mrs. Schlemiel would always say, "What a schlemiel! We will never have chickens on our chicken farm!" Mr. Schlemiel would retort back, "You will see! The chickens will be coming home to roost!"

Mrs. Schlemiel would then always shout back. "You can argue till the cows come home! The chickens will never be coming home to roost. You know why? The grass is greener on the other side of the road! Open your eyes! What a schlemiel!"

With no chickens and no cows, Mr. Schlemiel decided one day to see Mr. Schmegeggi and complain.

Mr. Schlemiel: Mr. Schmegeggi. The chickens have not come home to roost. When I argue with my wife that they will, she just tells me that I can argue till the cows come home. You have to help me here!

Mr. Schmegeggi: I anticipated this problem. So, I have brought with me this cow. Her name is Elsa. Bring her home, and you will never have to argue about the chickens coming home to roost again.

Mr. Schlemiel: Wonderful! Thank you so much! You have solved this problem!

Mr. Schlemiel went home with Elsa the Cow. He excitedly went to show his wife and the days of fighting were now over.

Mrs. Schlemiel: First of all, your scrawny little cow looks more like a goat. And second, I said "cows." Plural. You have one scrawny little goat cow. So, you can still argue till the cows come home! But I do have an idea. Why don't you take your scrawny little goat cow to the market, and maybe you can get a few dollars to buy some cheese. I can tell you that, by looking at your little cow, you are not going to get milk out of that thing.

Mr. Schlemiel disappointedly went to the market. He was immediately approached by a strange man who offered him magic seeds. Mr. Schlemiel was told that these seeds would grow the greenest grass in all the land. With the greenest grass in the land, the chickens would all then come home to roost.

Mr. Schlemiel then asked, "What if the seeds do not grow the grass?"

The strange man replied, "I give you a double your cow back guarantee! No grass and you get two cows!"

Mr. Schlemiel was very happy with this answer. Even if the grass did not grow, he would get two cows to come home. Plural. Cows. Mr. Schlemiel thought to himself that he would then never have to argue again.

Amazingly, these were indeed magic grass seeds. Months later, Mr. Schlemiel's farm had the greenest grass in all the land. Since the grass was now greener on his side of the road, all of the chickens had come home to roost. Even the cows, hearing about the delicious green grass, had come home as well.

Mr. Schlemiel, seeing all the chickens and cows on his farm, he excitedly ran to his wife.

Mr. Schlemiel: Isn't it wonderful! The chickens have come home to roost! And even the cows have come home!

Mrs. Schlemiel: So what! You know what I heard today at the market. You know our neighbor's son, Jack? He took their cow to the market and got beans. The beans grew a giant beanstalk. Guess what was at the top of the giant beanstalk? I will tell you. The goose that laid the golden egg!! And this kid, I think he is maybe ten years old, even defeated a giant at the top of the beanstalk. What a schlemiel you are!

This brings us to the most important thing to learn when you have to deal with Cows Come Home CrankaTsuris.

Sometimes, you can never win.

CHAPTER 30

AX TO GRIND
CRANKATSURIS

BEFORE I BEGIN TODAY'S LESSON on "Ax to Grind CrankaTsuris," which happens to be one of the most dangerous kinds of CrankaTsurises, I would like to start with a Yiddish lesson describing four types of characters:

Schlemiel. This is a Yiddish term meaning "incompetent person" or "fool" who always gets into unfortunate situations.

Schmegeggi. A contemptible person full of hot air and baloney.

Paskudnyak. A revolting sleaze ball. A nasty crooked and corrupt person.

Dreykop. Someone who talks nonstop and makes no sense. Someone who connives, twists, and distorts what may be the simplest logic.

I was watching television the other night, and a politician type of person was being interviewed. He mentioned that he had an "ax to grind." I found this to be a curious phrase. He was not holding any ax. He did not say why he needed to grind his ax, or what benefit he would be getting after grinding his ax. He did not even look like a person who even owned an ax.

Also, you will never hear anybody brag afterwards that they had successfully ground their ax. Imagine this conversation:

Partner One: Do you have anything special planned today at work?

Partner Two: Since you have mentioned it, I do. Today, I have an ax to grind!

Partner One: Well, that is good. Take some knives with you as well. They need some sharpening!

Later that day, Partner One comes home with what looks like an urn filled with ashes.

Partner One: Look what I have! (Holding up the urn) I ground the ax!

Partner Two: Where did you go? A crematorium?

Partner One: No. I used a special ax grinder.

Partner Two: An ax is not a coffee bean. How are we going to chop wood with a bunch of ax grounds? Why don't you take your ax grounds, and make yourself a cup of ax. When you are done, you can go out to the hardware store, and buy a new ax.

Partner One: Okay. But you do understand. For the longest time, I have been saying I have an ax to grind. It is now all ground. You should be happy!

Partner Two: (murmuring) What a schmuck.

Every day, more and more people are getting afflicted with Ax to Grind CrankaTsuris. You can go out and ask any person, and they will tell you that have many axes to grind. Because nobody has really ground an ax, this is a serious form of CrankaTsuris that must be dealt with. When you become afflicted with Ax to Grind CrankaTsuris, it takes the form of a singular thought in your head about how you have been personally dealt with a certain injustice.

It can also take form as a recurring argument in your head. It just spins around in your head, and it doesn't allow you to take any action on the injustice, or the argument. The mind becomes used to the injustice as a form of comfort or self-righteousness. You want to keep replaying the winning of the argument in your head. This then becomes a misplaced feeling of comfort, and you do not let go of this ax grinding feeling. You did not grind the ax, but you buried the hatchet inside your head.

As the Ax to Grind CrankaTsuris continues to consume the brain, the brain gets smaller and smaller until there is almost nothing left. Thus, it is important to know that no ax has ever been successfully ground up to make a positive difference. Because of this, if you catch yourself with the affliction of Ax to Grind CrankaTsuris, let the spinning thought go. Think of positive actions, and with this thought that is going nowhere, try to think of this as the time when you go and not bury, but rather remove this mental hatchet from your head.

This lesson can be learned from someone who is becoming a good teacher, Mr. Schlemiel. As you now know, Mr. Schlemiel bought a chicken farm from Mr. Schmegeggi. However, the chicken farm did not have any chickens. All of the chickens crossed the road to get to the other side. It was because the grass was always greener on the other side.

Mr. Schlemiel always was taken advantage of by other people. So, one day, Mr. Schlemiel hired the same Mr. Schmegeggi, who happened to be a lawyer, to sue all the people who ever took advantage of him.

Mr. Schlemiel was offered $5 million before the trial, $3 million during the trial, and $1 million just before the verdict came down. Every time, Mr. Schlemiel wanted to take the money. Every time, Mr. Schmegeggi told Mr. Schlemiel not to take the money. Of course, when the jury came back, Mr. Schlemiel was awarded nothing. He had lost the case.

Mr. Schlemiel then started calling Mr. Schmegeggi everyday afterwards for the next ten days. Every day, Mr. Schlemiel was told the same thing. Mr. Schmegeggi was very upset and very distraught over losing the case. He climbed to the top of the tallest building and jumped off the top of the tallest building. Mr. Schmegeggi was dead.

Mr. Schlemiel kept calling because he liked to hear the story. It gave him a bit of satisfaction and allowed him to move on with his life. So, one day, you can imagine the shock Mr. Schlemiel felt when he walked into the local market, and guess who he ran into? It was Mr. Schmegeggi.

Mr. Schlemiel felt waves of anger going through every ounce of his body, and he quickly ran up to confront Mr. Schmegeggi.

Mr. Schlemiel: Mr. Schmegeggi!!! What are you doing alive? I called you every day for almost two weeks, and every single day, they told me the same thing. They said you climbed to the top of the tallest building, and that you jumped off the top of the tallest building. They said that you were dead!

Mr. Schmegeggi: We had to tell you that story because we figured that you may have been a teensy-weensy bit upset that I lost your case.

Mr. Schlemiel: Teensy-weensy? I am furious! I could have had $5 million. Because of you, I have nothing! You are a good for nothing piece of!!!

Mr. Schmegeggi interrupted.

Mr. Schmegeggi: I had to lose the case. I had no choice.

Mr. Schlemiel: What do you mean you had to lose my case? What kind of lawyer are you?

Mr. Schmegeggi: Think about this. We were suing all the people who ever took advantage of you. I happened to be one of those people who took advantage of you. I did not want to win a case against myself!

Mr. Schlemiel: Ok. That makes a lot of sense. No. No. No. That sort of thing must be illegal! This sounds like you were acting in what has to be a clear conflict of interest!!!

Mr. Schmegeggi: It was a conflict for you. It was not a conflict for me.

Mr. Schlemiel: It is people like you who give lawyers a bad name.

Mr. Schmegeggi: (Switching the subject) Mr. Schlemiel. May I ask you a question? Do you happen to have an ax?

Mr. Schlemiel: Yes. I have an ax. Do you know why I have an ax? That stupid chicken farm without the chickens that you sold me also came without electricity. The only way I can keep the house warm is by chopping enough wood. But now, it is more than just wood I want to chop. Why do you ask?

Mr. Schmegeggi: I know how all of this can get resolved and you will feel much better. It sounds like to me that you have a very big ax to grind. This is what I will do. At my expense, I will have delivered to your chicken farm the highest quality ax grinder. Every day when you wake up, you will go out and grind the ax. If you keep grinding the ax, within a few months, you will feel much, much better, and all that anger you are holding inside yourself will be gone.

Mr. Schlemiel: You think that will work?

Mr. Schmegeggi: I can guarantee it!

Mr. Schlemiel: Well, thank you, Mr. Schmegeggi. You are not that bad a person after all. I will try this.

Sure enough, the ax grinder arrived at Mr. Schlemiel's chicken farm. Mr. Schlemiel woke up every morning, and diligently spent an hour everyday grinding the ax. However, the ax just became smaller and smaller until there was no ax left. By this time, it was already winter, and Mr. Schlemiel was found frozen by some local town folk in the corner of his home, covered in what looked like ax grounds.

Mr. Schlemiel was taken to the local hospital where they successfully defrosted him. The local town folk felt sorry for Mr. Schlemiel and started a GoFundMe page for Mr. Schlemiel, and they raised enough money to install electricity and both an air conditioning and heating system. Mr. Schlemiel would never have to grind an ax again.

They also helped Mr. Schlemiel find a good lawyer, and Mr. Schlemiel sued Mr. Schmegeggi and his law firm, Schmegeggi, Paskudnyak, and Dreykop, for all the times they took advantage of Mr. Schlemiel. The case went to a jury, and Mr. Schlemiel was awarded $10 million.

A few months later, Mr. Schlemiel was able to transform his chicken-less chicken farm to the largest chicken farm in the County. Mr. Schlemiel had the reputation of having the best chickens. Out of all the farms, he had the greenest grass in the County. Seeing this, all the chickens crossed the road to get to the side where Mr. Schlemiel's chicken farm stood.

A year later, Mr. Schlemiel, now the wealthiest man in town, thought he should call Mr. Schmegeggi, and try to bury the hatchet. But when he tried to call up the law firm, he only got this recording:

"The Law Firm of Schmegeggi, Paskudnyak, and Dreykop is now permanently closed. The three lawyers, all distraught and upset over losing a case, climbed to the top of the tallest building. They jumped off the top of the tallest building. Schmegeggi, Paskudnyak, and Dreykop are all dead."

Mr. Schlemiel hung up the phone and smiled. Giving a bit of a chuckle, he said out loud:

"I like to hear that story."

CHAPTER 31

First Rodeo
CrankaTsuris

PEOPLE ALWAYS LIKE TO BRAG, "This ain't my first rodeo." It always implies that the first rodeo was the most terrible and by far, the worst experience that this person ever experienced. You would not want to wish the first rodeo on your worst enemy. It always resulted in many broken bones, a severe concussion, and it was so traumatic that it required additional years of therapy. I hear that there are psychologists who are actually trained in this particular specialty to treat only those people who went to their first rodeo.

The question then becomes: "If the first rodeo was such a terrible and traumatizing experience, why even have a rodeo in the first place?" Perhaps, there should be a law passed that would ban all future rodeos.

There is another thing about these people who like to brag that "This ain't my first rodeo." They are telling the truth in one way. It is not their first rodeo because they have never been to a rodeo. In fact, they probably have not been within a thousand miles of the nearest rodeo. These braggarts don't even know the first thing about the rodeo.

Doctors, and in particular surgeons, who want to operate on me, always like to brag just as they are about to operate, "This ain't my first rodeo." I do not know about you, but if you ask me, personally, I would not be too thrilled if my brain surgeon told me, as he was about to open my cranium, that the brain operation ain't his or her first rodeo. I do not want a brain surgeon looking at my brain as if the brain surgeon was about to get on some bucking bronco.

This brain surgeon is staring at my brain, and the only thinking going on in the brain surgeon's own brain is about going to Pamplona, Spain to do the Running of the Bulls. Why? It happened to be on his "bucket list." I am sorry if I am a bit fussy, but when a brain surgeon operates on my brain, I want the brain surgeon to be solely focused on my brain.

The other interesting thing that I notice is how people who like to brag that "This ain't my first rodeo" do not have the same excitement when they say "This ain't my first circus."

Co-Worker One: So, what are you doing this weekend?

Co-Worker Two: I have to take all the kids to the circus. (He looks dismayed.)

Co-Worker One: That should be fun! But you do not look that excited.

Co-Worker Two: Well, this ain't my first circus.

Co-Worker One: Oh. I understand. Well, I hope you get through it.

Co-Worker Two: Thanks. Between the peanuts, the crackerjacks, and those circus lights they sell you, I guess I will survive.

If you are reading this, you may wonder how the origins of the saying "This ain't my first rodeo" even came about. Well, you are in luck because I happen to know the story how this line became famous.

There was a man named Mr. Schlemiel. Mr. Schlemiel, who was a real schlemiel, always had a dream of owning a chicken farm. He never could afford a chicken farm, but one day, he saw that a chicken farm became available at a price that he, Mr. Schlemiel, could afford. Mr. Schlemiel was so excited that he bought the chicken farm without even first taking a look at the farm.

It turned out for poor Mr. Schlemiel that the chicken farm had no chickens. It was the only chicken-less chicken farm in the County. Apparently, all the chickens had crossed the road to get to the other side. Mr. Schlemiel's farm was sitting right on top of a giant dust bowl, and no matter what Mr. Schlemiel did, the grass was always greener on the other side.

It was not very profitable to run a chicken farm without any chickens so Mr. Schlemiel, in order to earn some money, became desperate. He saw posted on a billboard nearby that a rodeo was opening up, and there was a "First Rodeo" competition with the winner getting $1000 as the First Prize.

Mr. Schlemiel was very excited, and he decided that he would enter the First Rodeo competition. He showed up behind all the other competitors who looked like big hulking men and who appeared to be real cowboys. Mr. Schlemiel just looked like a schlemiel.

Because of this, they put Mr. Schlemiel on Pippi the Prancing Pony. However, once Mr. Schlemiel got on Pippy, Pippy thought to himself "what a schlemiel." Pippi then put a bit of pep into his step, and poor Mr. Schlemiel fell off of Pippi. The handlers pulled Pippi away because he started to prance all over poor Mr. Schlemiel.

Though it resulted in a broken leg, Mr. Schlemiel was not deterred, and the following week, he showed up walking in crutches to enter the First Rodeo competition. This time, they decided to put Mr. Schlemiel on Dizzy the Dancing Donkey.

Once Mr. Schlemiel got onto Dizzy, Dizzy thought to herself, "what a schlemiel." Dizzy then started to spin like a spinning top that got Mr. Schlemiel so dizzy, Mr. Schlemiel fell off of Dizzy. Dizzy then grabbed Mr. Schlemiel by the collar of his shirt and started to disco dance, and bob his head up and down. Poor Mr. Schlemiel's head got bobbed up and down on the ground so hard that the rodeo handlers had to intervene and pull Dizzy away from Mr. Schlemiel.

Though it resulted in a severe concussion, and so many scrapes all over his face that it had to be bandaged, Mr. Schlemiel was not deterred. He showed up the next week, still walking with crutches, and his face all bandaged up. Again, Mr. Schlemiel signed up for the First Rodeo competition. This time, they decided to put Mr. Schlemiel on Kung-Fu, the Kicking Billy Goat.

Once Mr. Schlemiel got onto Kung-Fu, Kung-Fu thought to himself, "what a schlemiel." Kung-Fu then swung quickly around tossing poor Mr. Schlemiel to the ground. Kung-Fu then started to do Kung-Fu Kicks on Mr. Schlemiel that made a "chop–chop–chop" sound. Everyone could hear the bones in Mr. Schlemiel's arms make a cracking sound. It also appeared that a few of Mr. Schlemiel's teeth got kicked out as well. The rodeo handlers then came in and pulled Kung-Fu away from Mr. Schlemiel.

For the next six weeks, Mr. Schlemiel entered the First Rodeo competition, and every week, the result was the same. There were more broken bones, and it was so bad that Mr. Schlemiel was confined to a wheelchair. He now had to hire an aide to push him from one place to another.

Even though Mr. Schlemiel was now confined to a wheelchair, he was still not deterred, and sure enough, the following week, he once again showed up for the First Rodeo competition. The people who were running the rodeo were getting tired of Mr. Schlemiel showing up at the rodeo. They talked amongst themselves and decided that in order to get rid of him once and for all, they would enter Mr. Schlemiel in the Tenth Rodeo competition. Mr. Schlemiel was placed on Bully the Bucking Bronco who had the reputation of being the most dangerous bronco in the entire competition. Even the world champion bull riders had rarely been able to stay on Bully for more than thirty seconds, Poor Mr. Schlemiel would not last a second on Bully.

Once Mr. Schlemiel was placed on Bully, Bully thought to himself "what a schlemiel." Bully then went around the rodeo ring swinging back and forth, bucking up and down, and shook violently across the arena. However, no matter what Bully tried, Mr. Schlemiel would not fall off. Five minutes went by. Ten minutes went by. Mr. Schlemiel was still on Bully. Everyone started to stand up and cheer for Mr. Schlemiel, and amazingly enough, Mr. Schlemiel was the winner of the Tenth Rodeo competition.

Mr. Schlemiel, after being given his trophy, and the $10,000 prize money, was immediately surrounded by a group of reporters. They all wanted to know how Mr. Schlemiel was able to stay on Bully. Everyone could see Mr. Schlemiel crack a smile through his bandages, and he had just a few modest words to say.

"This ain't my first rodeo!"

Mr. Schlemiel became a crowd favorite, and he was no longer called Mr. Schlemiel. He became known as "Rodeo Joe" and after he retired, he was entered into the Rodeo Hall of Fame.

Because of his success at the rodeo, Mr. Schlemiel was able to buy a proper chicken farm with thousands of chickens. His farm was on the other side of the road where the grass was greener, because as we all know, the grass is always greener on the other side.

In finding our path to Effective Crankiness, we remind ourselves that we have all had the experience of our first rodeo. Some people, who are unfortunately ineffectively cranky, just keep going back to the same rodeo. However, with our CrankaTsuris Method, it slows down, and we take a close look. We become more mindful of what has happened. We think about the ways in which we can use more skillful means to deal with a particular cranky moment.

Then think about the feeling of "this ain't my first rodeo." It is a feeling of not being fazed, and not getting thrown off the bucking bronco. Of course, the bronco is still bucking. And of course this time, you are in complete control.

Once you feel confident that you can say "this ain't my first rodeo" you can finally find yourself on the other side. And as they say, it is true, the grass *is* always greener on the other side.

CHAPTER 32

CAN'T MAKE THIS STUFF UP CRANKATSURIS

NOW THAT I AM CONSIDERED TO BE A WRITER, I continually get asked the same question over and over again:

"Do you have a certain 'rule of thumb' that you follow when you write?"

I always have had difficulty giving an answer to that question. What does my thumb have to do with my writing? There are four other fingers. Do they get their own rule? Ok. I can understand not having a rule of the pinky. Nobody would take that rule very seriously. However, for someone who writes about crankiness, one could certainly imagine that the middle finger would get the "rule" award. Of course, that certainly would be much better than the "rule with an iron fist," or perhaps a "velvet glove." The middle finger knows how to make a point.

"Rule of thumb" is a phrase that many people use, but give little thought to where it came from, or think about whether it even makes any sense. We like to tell people about the "one good rule of thumb to follow." Yet, there is no such thing as a "bad rule of thumb."

I do remember, as a toddler, the thumb did have a special place in my heart, or actually, in my mouth. I would love to suck my thumb. I had no interest in any of the other fingers. If I got bored with one thumb, I would take it out of my mouth, and then stick the other one in my mouth, and happily started sucking away again.

Perhaps, that was where we came up with the phrase "rule of thumb." Of course, my parents had a different rule of thumb which was to keep the thumb out of my mouth. So maybe, that was where "rule of thumb" came from.

I started to research the origins, and surprisingly, it has nothing to do with thumb-sucking. According to Wikipedia, apparently, in 17th century England, a judge ruled that a husband was permitted to beat his wife as long as the stick that was used was no thicker than the man's thumb. There were also references to this "rule of thumb" in court opinions in the 1800s in both North Carolina and Mississippi.

Oy!!! And, Unbelievable.

As I was reading about the origins of the "rule of thumb" phrase, another phrase popped into my head that also needed some examination, in particular, when we look to how we can effectively manage our crankiness.

"You can't make this stuff up."

When I learned about the true origins of where the "rule of thumb" phrase came from, that was my reaction. "You can't make this stuff up." This reminded me that I have had the benefit of seeing many strange things happen during the course of my lifetime, and every time something weird happened, there was always one person who would make the same comment:

"You can't make this stuff up."

It then hit me. It is not the bizarre, strange and weird things that happen when it is appropriate to say "you can't make this stuff up." It is the exact opposite. We go day after day doing the exact same thing, dealing with the exact same stuff (or crap), and then, when a loved one asks you how your day was, the common response of many people is "Same Stuff (or Crap), Different Day." This then turns into another kind of CrankaTsuris that has to be dealt with. It is called "Can't Make This Stuff Up CrankaTsuris."

Think about it for a moment. It is another day. Your alarm goes off. You drag yourself out of bed. You make coffee. You get the kids ready for school. You then head off for work and deal with the same boss, the same customers, and the same headaches. You come home. You get dinner ready. You eat and clean up. You get the kids ready for bed. You then plop in front of the television. It is time to turn off the television. You then get ready for bed.

It is a day like this that I would have to make the comment:

"You can't make this stuff up."

Do you see now what I am saying? You string a few of those days together, and you are guaranteed to come down with a bad case of Can't Make This Stuff Up CrankaTsuris.

The cure to Can't Make This Stuff Up CrankaTsuris is rather simple and happens to be a lot of fun. All you have to do is spend some part of your day to make stuff up. Or, what you can do when you describe your lousy day is to just make stuff up!

Imagine how much fun it would be to have this family conversation:

Husband: How was your day today, honey? Or, let me ask it this way. Can you make stuff up?

Wife: After I dropped off Johnny at school, I got the truck onto the interstate to begin all my package deliveries. It was a freaking parking lot. Apparently, a chicken truck turned over, and all the chickens, who were still alive, escaped from the truck. There were hundreds of chickens crossing the road to get to the other side. Me, and a few other people, got out of our vehicles, and we all chased the chickens back in to the truck. If it wasn't for us doing that, I would still be sitting in traffic.

Husband: That was some day. I am impressed. You can make that stuff up.

Wife: I am not done. I may have delivered three packages at most, and then, I got a call from school. Little Johnny, our adorable five year old, was apparently reciting Shakespeare again during nap time. I was told that the teacher got scared again and that it would freak out the other kids. I had to take Johnny home. Johnny! Come here and tell your father what happened!

Johnny: You know that I want to be a Shakespearean actor when I grow up, so I was practicing Hamlet. It was nap time so I thought this would be appropriate:

> *"To be, or not to be: that is the question:*
> *Whether 'tis nobler in the mind to suffer*
> *The slings and arrows of outrageous fortune,*
> *Or to take arms against a sea of troubles,*
> *And by opposing end them? To die: to sleep;*
> *No more; and by a sleep to say we end*
> *The heart-ache and the thousand natural shocks*
> *That flesh is heir to, 'tis a consummation*
> *Devoutly to be wish'd. To die, to sleep;*
> *To sleep: perchance to dream: ay, there's the rub;*
> *For in that sleep of death what dreams may come*
> *When we have shuffled off this mortal coil,*
> *Must give us pause: there's the respect*
> *That makes calamity of so long life;*
> *For who would bear the whips and scorns of time,*
> *The oppressor's wrong, the proud man's contumely,*
> *The pangs of despis'd love, the law's delay,*
> *The insolence of office and the spurns."*

Husband: Johnny, didn't we tell you not to do Shakespeare in class. It scares the other kids.

Wife: That is not all that happened. When the teacher told Johnny to stop it, Johnny puts on his invisibility cloak, and everyone was scared that Johnny had run away.

Johnny: It is the teacher's fault. When I said, "To be or not to be: That is the question," the teacher said, "Not to be. That is the answer."

Wife: Actually, it was not all bad. Afterwards, I got calls from the other parents. It turns out that all the other kids loved Johnny doing Shakespeare. So, they are all getting together. Your son and the entire kindergarten class!! They will be performing Romeo and Juliet for the school play.

Husband: Wow. Now, I have to tell you something.

Wife: Yes. You can make stuff up!

Husband: Okay. I am not your husband, and Johnny, I am not your father. This morning, my people, or who you would refer to as aliens, abducted him. I am here on a temporary basis. My people are here to study the human species because we find you to be quite unusual. We will return him after we have completed our study.

Johnny: That is so cool! I can't wait to tell my friends!

Wife: You are an alien?

Husband: We would not refer to ourselves as aliens. In fact, we have met with people from many other planets, and we consider Earthlings the most alien creatures in the galaxy.

Wife: Hey! Why do you say that?

Husband: I understand that you and your husband work for the same company. You deliver boxes, and your husband boxes the boxes.

Wife: Yes. What is so alien about that?

Husband: And you both work for the richest person on the entire planet? Is that right?

Wife: Yeah. So what?

Husband: So, does he box a box or deliver any boxes?

Wife: No. Of course not. He gets in a spaceship and goes into outer space. That way, he can see all of us working.

Husband: I see. You Earthlings have a saying for something like this. I believe it is "You can't make this stuff up."

Wife: That is right. You can't make this stuff up.

Johnny: Wait a second! Didn't I do a great Hamlet? And, I am not even from another planet!

See. That was a lot of fun! I picked this particular Hamlet soliloquy because of the question "to be or not to be." Sometimes, we create stories to put us to sleep. But, it is just as important to tell stories to wake us up. It is time to wake up! Try to spend a bit of time everyday doing something creative or take all the stuff that you really can't make up, and start adding in all the stuff you can make up. You made a cup of coffee? How about getting bitten by a radioactive spider at the same time? Didn't feel like cooking dinner? Well, a fairy godmother came and delivered fresh pizza! Go to town and be a bit crazy! Get yourself abducted by an alien or two.

Now, this is not meant to be training so you get to proudly call yourself the world's greatest pathological liar. This is about enriching ourselves with stories that light up our own and each other's lives. We all have the ability to really make this stuff up! We all get a chance to be! That is the answer!

Hey! I think I found myself a new "rule of thumb"!

Or perhaps the cure to Can't Make This Stuff Up Cranka Tsuris.

CHAPTER 33

DON'T GET ME STARTED
CRANKATSURIS

WE HAVE EXAMINED ALL DIFFERENT FORMS OF CRANKATSURISES. Some are very common and easily treatable. Others are much more serious and require serious intervention. One of the more dangerous CrankaTsuris that a person can become afflicted with is called Don't Get Me Started CrankaTsuris.

The person who suffers from this particular form of CrankaTsuris actually keeps the CrankaTsuris inside, and does not share the

CrankaTsuris with his or her closest friends or family members. The CrankaTsuris is not let out, but rather, it is eating up this person inside. You may notice a friend or relative with this disabling CrankaTsuris just sitting alone in a corner, talking to him or herself. When it gets this serious, they also have "I Am Beside Myself CrankaTsuris." This is easy to detect just by the fact that they have decided that the only ones they want to have conversations with are themselves.

As previously disclosed, many years ago, my neighbors were the Barkers. Just to refresh our recollection, the Barker family was made up of Woody and Maple Barker, and their two kids, Birch and Willow. All of the family members had lost their voice after they each would just tell each other that "you are barking up the wrong tree."

Finally, they went to see Dr. Sylvia Burt, who happened to be a Barking up the Right Tree specialist. After months of working with the Barkers, all of their voices came back. They learned how to bark up the right tree.

My other neighbors were a couple, Harry, and Sally Non-Starter. When Harry met Sally, there had been an instant connection. They would share every aspect of their day, and their most intimate secrets. However, years later, their relationship fell apart and they became distant from one another. If one partner asked the other the simple question of "what is the matter?" the reply was always the same.

"Don't get me started!"

The Non-Starters heard how Dr. Burt helped the Barkers, and because of their own desperate situation, they called up Dr. Burt and made their own appointment.

They came in the next morning, and after Harry and Sally got comfortable, Dr. Burt turned to both Harry and Sally, and asked:

"Who wants to start?"

Harry and Sally both responded quickly as if each one had the same nervous tick.

"Don't get me started!"

Dr. Burt then replied, "Excellent. Then, I will get started."

Dr. Burt began to speak:

You are both suffering from Don't Get Me Started CrankaTsuris. However, this is from having a number of other CrankaTsurises that we have to unwrap.

While this is therapy, you have to break everything down as if you are both lawyers. Now, while most people are not lawyers, they litigate their lives and misfortunes in their head, except that it becomes a loop that just repeats itself. Together, we will break this loop that has become your own personal addiction. You do not want to share this addiction, and that is why you both suffer from Don't Get Me Started CrankaTsuris, and at times, I am Beside Myself CrankaTsuris.

This stems from the many grievances you have, and we all have them. Nobody is immune. We will put a particular grievance into the form of a trial. But, to make you see how this works, we only look at the opening statement and closing argument of a trial. We can skip everything in the middle because it is these two parts of the trial that your brain focuses on.

The opening statement is when you describe what the evidence will show. Think about this as the promises you will make to a jury. You happen to be your own jury as well. You consider these promises to be "airtight, rock-solid, and iron-clad."

The closing argument is when you tell the jury that this case is your favorite case to try. It is not because of fancy experts, or sexy issues. It is because you can rely on the common sense of the jury. Whenever you can rely on the common sense of the jury, juries always do the right thing.

Now, think of the situation litigating in your head that you have convinced yourself that you have both the promises you can keep, and the common sense as to what the outcome will be. Not only that, but you happen to be correct. Yet, the outcome is not what you expected. That is what is called "Rant and Rave CrankaTsuris." You are furious of this complete injustice.

The next case is when you can make some promises, and the other party in a dispute can make some too. While you can create a story that has common sense, the other party can as well. That is called "Bitch and Moan CrankaTsuris."

Again, you do not get the result you hoped for. You are angry, and you try to create maybe a different story, or a different trial that may have ended up better. You are in the re-trial loop.

The third case is when you have less to promise, and you have a very tough opposing counsel. You certainly do not get the result you desire. Here, it is called "Hem and Haw CrankaTsuris."

You can understand why you lost the case. However, it leaves a bad taste in your mouth. You are not happy.

The last case is when you just know you have a loser case, and you are not very happy about that. You even understand the outcome. This is called "Mumble and Grumble CrankaTsuris." Imagine that you are playing poker, and just got dealt a very bad hand.

We need to be able to separate each of these CrankaTsurises, but most importantly, we have to be aware of the most difficult one of these four, the Rant and Rave CrankaTsuris. Harry, when you met Sally, there may have been little to rant and rave about, and the same for you, Sally, except for the love you had for each other.

What we do here is learn how to bark up the right tree. When each of you experiences Rant and Rave CrankaTsuris, or even the other three, you both have to commit to being the right tree to bark up. You both get to be compassionate listeners, and when needed, problem-solvers as well.

With any of these four types of CrankaTsuris, they all have a story with a less than desired outcome. They are each the case you had litigating in your head. Together, you can both figure out a new case with no guaranteed outcome, but it will be one that gets you both started.

This ultimately is the cure to Don't Get Me Started CrankaTsuris.

Harry and Sally changed their last name to the "Starters." Nine months later, they had a beautiful baby Starter. They both learned that "starting" is something you just might need to do every day.

It turns out that when you don't want to get started, it just happens to be the perfect time to start!

CHAPTER 34

ROCKET SCIENCE CRANKATSURIS

ALL THE KING'S HORSES AND ALL THE KING'S MEN couldn't put Humpty Dumpty back together again. When the men and the horses arrived back at the castle, and they explained to both the King and the Queen that they had failed in their mission, both the King and Queen responded in disgusted disbelief.

"You know, this isn't rocket science!" said the King.

"You know, this isn't brain surgery!" said the Queen. "And tell me again. Why did we need all those horses?" asked the Queen.

While it was quite complicated to actually put Humpty Dumpty's eggshell body back together again, these two phrases continued on and have been used by many over the centuries. However, rather than making these comments over complicated tasks, they have been used more often when a person fails in the simplest of tasks. This ends up creating what is called "Rocket Science CrankaTsuris."

While this type of CrankaTsuris may be fleeting for the person who makes the criticism, it is a more dangerous form of CrankaTsuris for the person who has received it. This person, who is being told essentially that he or she has failed in the simplest of tasks, may then be afflicted with a "Why Bother to Do Anything? CrankaTsuris," and that may result in long lasting and unintended consequences.

We learn this lesson in the continuing saga of Herbie Snoodleman and Sour Croodleman. This was in a world where the sky was always blue, and the air was always clean. Everyone was always happy. Everybody loved their Snoodle which ran on noodles, and not only was it the preferred mode of transportation, it also provided everyone with a delicious dinner when they came home from a long day of work.

The Snoodle, which was the brainchild of Herbie Snoodleman, replaced the KrautMobile. The KrautMobile had been invented by Sour Croodleman, and ran solely on sauerkraut. This made the KrautMobile rather stinky, and everyone particularly cranky. However, when the Snoodle took over, Sour Croodleman quickly went out of business.

Sour did open up a very successful café called the Weiner Schnoodle Café. It was named after a poodle named Schnoodle soon after Sour discovered that poodles loved sauerkraut. Sour even got his own poodle named Schmoodle, who was the happiest poodle on the planet. You see. Schmoodle was provided with an endless supply of sauerkraut.

What was not known to the general public was the fact that Herbie Snoodleman and Sour Croodleman were actually brothers. Sour stopped talking to Herbie after Herbie's Snoodle Empire put the Sour KrautMobile Empire out of business, and for a while, also made him quite an unpopular figure.

Herbie and Sour had a third brother. His name was Norman Noodle. Norman Noodle and his wife, Sally Stroodle, ran the most popular pastry shop in all the land. It was called the From the Noodle Comes the Stroodle Patisserie, and it featured Norman's Noodle Pie, and Sally's delicious Stroodle Noodle Cake.

They had two kids. Their daughter was named Briana Brainy Broodle. Their son was named Ricky Rockadoodle.

The parents tried to teach their kids the secrets to making delicious pies and cakes out of noodles. But no matter how many times they tried, the kids showed no interest, and could not ever get it right. Sally Stroodle would complain to Briana Brainy Broodle, "You know. This isn't brain surgery!" Norman Noodle would scold Ricky Rockadoodle, "You know. This isn't rocket science!"

In fact, this became the two common refrains in the Noodle Stroodle household. If any task was not completed to their full satisfaction, Sally Stroodle would say "You know. This isn't brain surgery!" Norman Noodle would say "You know. This isn't rocket science!"

However, Briana Brainy Broodle's true passion was brain surgery. Ricky Rockadoodle was very interested in rocket science. They also had two of the best teachers: their two Uncles Herbie Snoodleman and Sour Croodleman.

Brianna would go to her Uncle Herbie's house, and he would explain how he came about to inventing the Snoodle.

Herbie Snoodleman: For years, I did all these brain operations. I finally realized that the brain was not so different than a bowl of macaroni and cheese. I also realized that when people said that they were using their noodle, they were really talking about brain power. I then thought if noodles provide the intelligence for our brains, perhaps, it can be applied to modes of transportation. After years in my laboratory, the Snoodle was born. It is because the noodle brain detects the smell of noodles in the air, the Snoodle provides the ultimate happiness.

Briana Brainy Broodle: One day, I want to be a great brain surgeon like you!

Herbie Snoodleman: Thank you, my dear. Right now, I am working on a Snoodle that can achieve space travel. I call it the Snoodle Zoomadoodle. While it can go past the Earth's atmosphere, unfortunately, I have not been able to create the necessary speed to achieve travel into other galaxies.

Brianna comforted her uncle with a hug. "You can do anything, Uncle Herbie!"

Ricky Rockadoodle would love to visit his Uncle Sour at the Weiner Schnoodle Café. When the café was closed, Uncle Sour would take Ricky Rockadoodle to the back of his café, and show off his next great invention.

Sour Croodleman: This is my greatest invention ever! I call it the Prickly Peppered Purple Propulsion Powered Pickle! I started with just a simple Propulsion Powered Pickle which you can just stick in any Snoodle. But, with the Prickly Peppered Purple Propulsion Powered Pickle, we can achieve space travel ten times faster than the speed of light! Think of it! We will now be able explore galaxies far beyond our own. Unfortunately, there is just one little problem.

Ricky Rockadoodle: What is the problem, Uncle Sour?

Sour Croodleman: In my tests, the Prickly Peppered Purple Propulsion Powered Pickle will only work with a Snoodle-type vehicle. And, no matter what, I will never work with that brother of mine after what he did to my reputation.

Ricky Rockadoodle: Well, I think you are the Cooldleman of the two uncles, and one day, I will be a great rocket scientist just like you.

Sour Croodleman beamed as he was feeding his poodle, Schmoodle, a bowl of sauerkraut.

One day, Briana Brainy Broodle and Ricky Rockadoodle came home from school, and found a note waiting for them at home. It said:

We have abducted your parents, and they are now safe on our spaceship, the Zoodle Kidoodle. We are from the planet, Zoodle. Once your parents perform brain surgery on our leader, Cloodle the Grand Roodle, and make repairs to our rockets on the Zoodle Kidoodle Spaceship, they will be returned safe and sound. Meanwhile, you can observe your parents by simply going to our website — www.Zoodle.gov/the abduction/livestream.

Sincerely yours,

Evil Kidoodle

PS. Your mom says that there is Stroodle Noodle Cake in the fridge.

Meanwhile, on the Zoodle Kidoodle, Evil Kidoodle was welcoming Norman Noodle and Sally Stroodle.

Evil Kidoodle: You are now on our spaceship, the Zoodle Kidoodle. My name is Evil Kidoodle. My associates here are Voodoo Kidoodle, DooDoo Kidoodle, and Doctor Quack Kidoodle. The reason we brought you here is, that for centuries, the Zoodles had the greatest brain surgeons and rocket scientists in the galaxy. Unfortunately, they were proud and a bit arrogant. When they looked at anyone else's accomplishments, they would just poo-poo and say "You know. It isn't brain surgery." and "You know. It isn't rocket science." Soon, everyone became afraid to become brain surgeons or rocket scientists, and now unfortunately, we have none left.

Norman Noodle: What does that have to do with us?

Evil Kidoodle: We have monitored many planets, and we learned that both of you like to say the same thing about brain surgery and rocket scientists. So, we determined that you two, just like on our planet centuries ago, possess the knowledge of brain surgery and rocket science. The rockets on our spaceship are failing and we cannot return to Zoodle until they are fixed.

Doctor Quack Kidoodle: Also, our great leader, Cloodle the Grand Roodle, unfortunately has come down with a rare disease of the brain. It is called Genius Brain. This is similar to what you humans may call athlete's feet. It is a fungus on the brain. First, the person afflicted shows superior genius mental powers but the brain then just fizzles out. I am afraid that Cloodle the Grand Roodle of the planet Zoodle is now just a Wackadoodle. Here. You can both view him on the giant monitor. You can see him in the rubber room of our spaceship.

Cloodle the Grand Roodle did appear to be a bit of a Wackadoodle. He was just sitting on the floor dressed in diapers, doodling with crayons, and just muttering "bah, bah, bah, bah."

Sally Stroodle: But we do not know anything about brain surgery or rocket science. We are just simple bakers! It is just a saying we use. You have to let us go. You made a big mistake!

Evil Kidoodle: We thought you may be reluctant. This is why we have placed above over the atmosphere of your planet Earth eight giant Vacuudoodles. We use Vacuudoodles to vacuum valuable resources from other planets that allow Zoodles to thrive. We have put a setting on the Vacuudoodles to vacuum all of the noodles on your planet until it is left completely and utterly noodle-less. Unless you agree to comply, we will begin the noodle vacuudoodle process in 48 hours. And for the fate of you two, Voodoo Kidoodle will explain.

Voodoo Kidoodle: I have two dolls. One is named Norman Noodle. The other, I have named Sally Stroodle. I have in my hand a wet noodle. I take this wet noodle and go tickle, tickle, tickle.

Both Norman Noodle and Sally Stroodle started to laugh uncontrollably. Voodoo Kidoodle then abruptly stopped. The laughing stopped as well.

Voodoo Kidoodle: Now, if you do not comply, I have some spaghetti that is uncooked and a quite a bit stiff. If I poke the spaghetti through the two dolls, both of you will be feeling a bit more than just heartburn.

Norman Noodle: You got us. I am a rocket scientist and Sally is in fact a brain surgeon. But we are not the most brilliant.

Sally Stroodle: Norman, what are you saying?

Norman: Excuse my wife. While we both possess the knowledge, we are not the best. We also need both tools and assistance. We have to summon our two kids, and my two brothers, Herbie Snoodleman, and Sour Croodleman. They have some new technology that even we do not know about. You deserve only the best. I assure you. They are the best you can find in the galaxy.

Evil Croodleman: We will give you back your phones, and you can make contact. They can come up to our spaceship in a Snoodle equipped for space travel. But they have to arrive in 48 hours. Also, you may ask: "What is that awful smell?"

Sally Stroodle: It did cross our mind.

Evil Kidoodle: It is DooDoo Kidoodle. DooDoo does not do much, but we Zoodles like the smell. We understand that, for Earthlings, he smells a bit like DooDoo. DooDoo Kidoodle will stand on guard.

After three of the Zoodles left the room, even before they were able to call their kids, Briana Brainy Broodle and Ricky Rockadoodle called their parents.

Briana Brainy Broodle: We saw everything on the Livestream. I am going over right now to Uncle Herbie. Ricky will go over to Uncle

Sour. With the planet at stake, we will get them back together and be up with you in a flash.

Ricky Rockadoodle: Uncle Sour will go for this. With the Prickly Peppered Purple Propulsion Powered Pickle, we will zoom to the Zoodle Kidoodle in no time!

Sally Stroodle: Please hurry! It smells like a big doo doo up here!!

Briana Brainy Broodle and Ricky Rockadoodle quickly sped off in their KidSnoodles to see their uncles.

Ricky Rockadoodle explained the situation to his Uncle Sour. A big gleeful smile emerged on his face.

Sour Croodleman: The planet completely and utterly noodle-less? What joy! I finally get my sour revenge! I will be able to sell Krautmobiles like hot noodle cakes!

Ricky Rockadoodle: What about my parents? And just think. You will make history with space travel, not to mention saving the planet!!

Sour Croodleman reflected for a second and turned to Ricky Rockadoodle.

Sour Croodleman: What are you waiting for? Grab a jar of prickly purple pickles from the fridge!

Briana Brainy Broodle explained the dire situation to her Uncle Herbie.

Herbie Snoodleman: I am afraid to say that the only way we can get up to the Zoodle Kidooodle Spaceship in time is if we can get a Snoodle powered with the Prickly Peppered Purple Propulsion Powered Pickle, I understand your Uncle Sour just invented. Your Uncle Sour will never agree to help.

At that moment, there was a knock at the door. Sure enough, there stood Ricky Rockadoodle, Sour Croodleman, and his poodle, Schmoodle.

Sour Croodleman: I hear that somebody needs some pickles for a little trip. I also packed some sandwiches!

Together with Schmoodle the Poodle, the four ran out to the special Snoodle that was developed for space travel. Sour Croodleman inserted one of his special prickly purple pickles, and in a flash, they blasted off into space and quickly were able to land on the Zoodle Kidoodle.

Herbie Snoodleman and Briana Brainy Broodle were led to see Cloodle the Grand Roodle of the planet Zoodle. A table was set up and Cloodle the Grand Roodle was placed on the table. Herbie Snoodleman turned to Briana Brainy Broodle.

Herbie Snoodleman: You will do this operation.

Briana Brainy Broodle: Only with you help, Uncle Herbie!

They opened up Cloodle the Roodle's head, and they quickly went to work. Briana Brainy Broodle was in control.

Briana Brainy Broodle: Linguini.

Briana Brainy Broodle: A few raviolis.

Briana Brainy Broodle: A bowl of macaroni and cheese.

Briana Brainy Broodle: Angel hair for the stitching.

After a couple of hours, Cloodle the Grand Roodle was all stitched up and resting.

Meanwhile, in the engineering room of the spaceship, Ricky Rockadoodle and Sour Croodleman were both fast at work.

Ricky Rockadoodle: I followed exactly what you told me. Hey! It turns out that the Zoodle Kidoodle Spaceship runs on a fuel that combines both noodles and sauerkraut! I will now screw on the Prickly Pickle Adapter. And the jalapeno peppers made this pickle particularly purple and prickly! It's going to work!

Sour Croodleman: I am so proud of you!! You sound like a real rocket scientist!

After the success of Briana Brainy Broodle and Ricky Rockadoodle, everyone was united together where Norman Noodle and Sally Stroodle were being held captive. There were hugs all around. However, this was interrupted when all the Zoodles entered the room led by Cloodle the Grand Roodle of the planet Zoodle.

Cloodle the Grand Roodle: I want to personally thank you for successfully repairing my brain. Our engineers have checked the engines with the prickly purple peppered pickles you put installed and have advised us that we are now able to go back to our planet, Zoodle. We have now removed the Vacuudoodles from the Earth's atmosphere, and the Earth can keep all of its noodles.

Norman Noodle: So, we can all go home now.

Cloodle the Grand Roodle: I am afraid that is not possible. You see. We will need your services to help train other Zoodles to be brain surgeons and rocket scientists. Plus, I did get a chance to taste both the noodle pie and the stroodle noodle cake. They were both so delicious. We will need training for that as well.

Sally Stroodle: How long will you require us to perform this training?

Cloodle the Grand Roodle: It will not be long. After 100 years, we will return all of you back to your planet.

Briana and Ricky: 100 years!!! We will miss out on high school!!

Cloodle the Grand Roodle: Except for the Poodle named Schmoodle. You see. On the planet Zoodle, we do not allow pets.

Cloodle the Grand Roodle then turned to DooDoo Kidoodle and instructed to take Schmoodle the Poodle and put him back in the Snoodle. DooDoo Kidoodle then picked up Schmoodle the Poodle. However, Schmoodle the Poodle loved the smell of DooDoo Kidoodle. Once he was picked up, Schmoodle the Poodle started licking DooDoo Kidoodle uncontrollably. Schmoodle the Poodle then jumped out of DooDoo Kidoodle's arms and started going into a spinning happy dance.

Fumes of sauerkraut coming from Schmoodle the Poodle formed into a cloud over the Zoodles. All the Zoodles, who were not used to the smell of sauerkraut, quickly all fell asleep.

Sour Croodleman: That's a good Schmoodle!

Herbie Snoodleman: Back to the Snoodle!

They all jumped into the Snoodle, and before any of the Zoodles regained consciousness, they escaped from the Zoodle Kidoodle Spaceship, and were quickly back on Earth.

Two weeks later, Briana Brainy Broodle and Ricky Rockadoodle were both presented with keys to the city for their heroism in saving the planet.

When asked whether they found it difficult to save a planet, Briana Brainy Broodle simply said "It was a piece of cake!" Ricky Rockadoodle followed up with "It was easy as pie!"

Then, someone asked where Herbie Snoodleman and Sour Croodleman were. Nobody knew exactly.

You see. Herbie Snoodleman and Sour Croodleman were already back in space together on their next great adventure!

CHAPTER 35

PEANUT GALLERY CRANKATSURIS

WHEN I WAS A TEENAGER, I went to my first rock concert. It was back in 1975 at Madison Square Garden, and it wasn't just any concert. It was Paul McCartney and Wings. I was going to see an ex–Beatle. It didn't matter where I was sitting. I was in the arena! The buildup started blocks away when you had hordes of scalpers looking to sell tickets, and desperate fans looking to buy. Vendors seemed to grow right out of the sidewalk selling "Wings over America" t-shirts. On top of all this buildup, all my friends (myself included) had the fantasy that Paul would invite John, George and Ringo on stage, and there would be a Beatles reunion. Where else would they do such a thing other than Madison Square Garden?

Of course, the seats were up in the nosebleed section. These are the seats that are so high up that everybody's noses start to bleed. Not only were we so far up that we could not really see anything, but our view was further diminished because we were all holding their head back with tissues in their noses trying to stop the bleeding.

Despite the fact that every single person in the "nosebleed" section each lost three pints of blood during the concert, there was not a single person that complained. We all knew we were going to sit in those seats and we made the decision to buy the seats anyway. We just wanted to be in the building. Only our parents suffered from Nosebleed CrankaTsuris. This was because, after three hours of bloodletting, a lot of the blood did manage to get on our shirts and pants. All the parents looked at their kids in horror as though they had come back from a gang war.

"Peanut Gallery CrankaTsuris" is a bit different and is a CrankaTsuris that is worth looking at. There are many historical references to the term "Peanut Gallery" but similar to the "Nosebleed" seats, the "Peanut Gallery" are the seats all the way up in the upper balcony. This term goes all the way back to the 19th century. When people sat in these seats, they could not really see or hear what was going on down at the stage. The people on stage may have looked like peanuts, but the term was used because peanuts were sold by the theater and the unlucky patrons who sat in these seats would heckle and throw peanuts at the performers on stage. Apparently, the people who sat in these seats were very capable peanut throwers, and probably had trained particularly just for such an occasion.

The "Peanut Gallery" phrase was also referred to in racial terms. Again, going back to the 19th Century, in many theaters, African Americans could only sit in the upper balcony of the theater, and this as well was referred to as the "Peanut Gallery."

This is a form of CrankaTsuris because these people sitting up in the Peanut Gallery could not see or hear exactly what was going on.

Despite this, they made the judgment that the performers were all lousy, and these attendees up in the cheap seats had thus earned the right to give the performers their opinion by pelting them with peanuts. In the second use of this phrase, the judgment was made about the people who had to sit in this section.

This is exactly why we need to examine this particular kind of CrankaTsuris. Even though we are not sitting in a theater, we take in and try to process so much information every day, we all end up making judgments based on incomplete information. We decide before we see. We decide before we hear. The rush to judgment then becomes a CrankaTsuris for the person dishing it out, and it is a CrankaTsuris for the unfortunate person on the receiving end. It then becomes likely that there will be a CrankaTsuris retaliation, and the entire interaction can turn into a Peanut Gallery CrankaTsuris food fight.

Years ago, I lived in a town that featured one wealthy family as the most beloved in the entire town. They were generous and caring and it never mattered what a stranger looked like, or where they may have come from. However, it had not always been like that. For years, the parents, in particular, thought that they were special and better than everyone else. Why not think like that? They were the 'Fancy Nuts' family. They were a family of four. Petey Pecan was the father. Patty Pistachio was the mom. Their two kids were named Chrissy Cashew and Mickey Macadamia.

Chrissy Cashew and Mickey Macadamia did not have the same attitude as their parents. They liked to play with all of the other kid nuts in town, and they were both very excited when they got major roles in the local production of *The Nutcracker*. Chrissy Cashew got to play the Sugarplum Fairy. Mickey Macadamia got picked to play the Mouse King.

There was one problem for Chrissy Cashew and Mickey Macadamia. The rest of the cast were all ordinary peanuts, and they knew that their parents would not approve of them performing with peanuts when the family had a reputation of being the "Fancy Nuts."

Because of this, Chrissy Cashew and Mickey Macadamia hatched a plan to use fake peanut name aliases in the program. Chrissy Cashew was named "Penny Peanut." Mickey Macadamia named himself "Paulie Peanut." They would get tickets for their parents up in the Peanut Gallery so the parents would not be able to tell who they really were. Chrissy Cashew and Mickey Macadamia would then let their parents know they were actually in the production.

The night of the performance, Petey Pecan and Patty Pistachio had their driver take them to the Every Nut Theater where *The Nutcracker* performance was going to be held. Both Petey Pecan and Patty Pistachio were outraged when they found out that their seats were up in the Peanut Gallery. The performance was sold out so they could not exchange the tickets to a section where perhaps Fancy Nuts were seated. Once seated, everyone in the Peanut Gallery were peanuts themselves. Petey Pecan and Patty Pistachio were each given a bag of peanuts and shown to their seats.

> Petey Pecan: Can you believe this? What is the world coming to when Fancy Nuts like us have to sit in the Peanut Gallery. Do you have a program? I want to see Chrissy Cashew and Mickey Macadamia in the program. We surely won't be able to see them perform on stage.

> Patty Pistachio: I do not see them listed in the program! They are all Peanuts. Do you think it is a mistake?

> Petey Pecan: They are Peanuts. You know how Peanuts are. They probably left out all the Fancy Nuts out of the program intentionally. You know what. They gave us each a bag of peanuts. When the show begins, if we do not see our kids, we will just toss the peanuts at the stage. We Fancy Nuts shouldn't be forced to sit through this!

> Patty Pistachio: Sounds like fun! Petey Pecan. You certainly are the fanciest nut around!

> Petey Pecan: Touché!

As the lights dimmed, and the curtains rose up, the audience were instructed to turn off their cell phones. However, they were not instructed what to do with their bag of peanuts. Sure enough, once the performance started, both Petey Pecan and Patty Pistachio started to fling their peanuts at the stage. The performance was quickly stopped. Sensing that they could both be in trouble, Petey Pecan and Patty Pistachio slipped out of the theater before they were caught.

That night, both Chrissy Cashew and Mickey Macadamia came home crying and their faces both swollen.

Patty Pistachio: What happened to you two kids?

Chrissy Cashew: We both got hit by flying peanuts. Apparently, there was somebody in the Peanut Gallery throwing peanuts at the stage.

Mickey Macadamia: The police are looking for any information on who they could be. Were you there? Did you see who did it?

Petey Pecan: Ummm… Ummm. We didn't see you in the program.

Patty Pistachio: Yes. We didn't see you in the program, and we were not accustomed to sitting up in the Peanut Gallery. It is not something Fancy Nuts do. So, we left.

Chrissy Cashew: We were afraid that you would not approve of us performing with Peanuts. We took on Peanut names. I was Penny Peanut and Mickey Macadamia was Paulie Peanut.

Mickey Macadamia: But because we were hit with peanuts, the other Peanuts in the cast gave us first row seats for tomorrow's performance. We have to show that we are not intimidated by those hecklers up in the Peanut Gallery. You will come to watch us?

Patty Pistachio: Of course, we will watch you. It is true that we would not have approved you both performing with Peanuts, but you are our children. We will be there!

Petey Pecan: First Row!! I will contact the theater to make sure only Fancy Nuts are served. Nobody would ever throw a Fancy Nut. They are too delicious. Not to mention expensive. The Peanuts wouldn't even be able to afford them.

Chrissy and Mickey: Dad!! Peanuts are just as good as any Fancy Nut!

The next day, Petey Pecan and Patty Pistachio arrived at the theater. They sat in the seats that they were more accustomed to. However, this was going to be their first performance that featured Peanuts. While they were not expecting much, except for their own children of course, they were mesmerized by the dance and music. Tears ran down both Petey Pecan and Patty Pistachio's eyes. When the show was over, they gave both of their children the biggest hugs.

The next month, Petey Pecan and Patty Pistachio broke ground for the building of the town's new museum. It was called the Peanut Performance Museum of Visual Arts and Gallery. Featuring works of art from the likes of Pablo Peanut Picasso and Jackson Peanut Pollock, it quickly became the hottest ticket in town.

Getting back to our look at Peanut Gallery CrankaTsuris, this certainly does not mean that when we look closely, we will be guaranteed something of beauty and that will surely move us. We may decide that up close, it is even worth tossing an egg or a tomato. Hopefully not. But when everyone is looking closely, with an open mind, the focus is on the respectful exchange of ideas. When we can have that as the focus with our opened minds, we then hit upon the cure for the Peanut Gallery CrankaTsuris.

CHAPTER 36

FINAL STRAW CRANKATSURIS

IN *A GROWNUP GUIDE TO EFFECTIVE CRANKINESS,* one chapter was titled "The Straw that Broke the Camel's Back CrankaTsuris." The point of that story was to acknowledge the fact that we all go through life carrying various amounts of straw. In fact, we should not react to every straw as being the "final straw." If we let out a CrankaTsuris every time we are confronted with a single straw, life would become rather difficult rather quickly.

However, when we examine "Final Straw CrankaTsuris," we understand that this is a terrible CrankaTsuris that we should always work to avoid. This is completely different from the straw that broke the camel's back. The only way that we can really find the solution to Final Straw CrankaTsuris is by closely looking at each of these straws. Getting back to The Straw that Broke the Camel's Back CrankaTsuris story, there was a camel named Camel that had no problem with carrying bundles of straw, but unfortunately, one straw meant for a can of Pepsi broke Camel's back.

But, in reality, every straw always has the potential to be the Final Straw.

This particular kind of straw occurs when somebody close to you, typically a family member or friend, gives you his or her word. You rely upon what this person has promised, but of course, the promise ends up being broken. You even instruct this person not to make promises that he or she does not intend to keep. Despite this, you are reassured. There is the old saying "Fool me once, shame on you! Fool me twice, shame on me!"

Now, imagine if you have been fooled hundreds of times, and you keep all of that disappointment inside, or you gently nag the person who gave you his or her word. By the time you hit a thousand, it becomes the final straw. We want to avoid not only the thousandth time. We want to avoid the first time. Is this even possible?

Luckily, for you readers, I have come across highly confidential and classified government documents from the 1960s. It was sitting in a box, just gathering dust in my friend's basement. He said that he had bought it at a yard sale. Some of these documents are unbelievably fascinating and can actually help us deal with Final Straw CrankaTsuris.

I am sure that everyone, or mostly everyone, has watched Star Trek one time or another. However, what you do not know is that all of the stories are true. The Starship Enterprise traveled back in time to the past, and they gave the US Government their travel journals hoping that they could learn valuable lessons moving into the future.

One of the more interesting reads was the recorded interview between Captain Kirk and Mr. Spock. Mr. Spock was interviewing for the position of First Officer.

Captain Kirk: Mr. Spock. Your resume is outstanding, and your reputation is known far beyond this galaxy. However, I have one important question. Can you give me your word that you will be completely loyal to my command and the mission of the Federation?

Mr. Spock: Captain. I am clearly interested in the position of First Officer. I intend to be loyal and trustworthy. You can be assured of this fact. However, I cannot give you my word that I will be loyal to your command and the mission of the Federation. To do that would be highly illogical.

Captain Kirk: Mr. Spock. I find your reasoning to be highly illogical. You should know that I have interviewed over twenty other candidates, and I can tell you that every single candidate has given their word that they would be completely loyal and trustworthy.

Mr. Spock: And you should know that I would be far more loyal and trustworthy than any of these candidates.

Captain Kirk: Explain. I am interested in hearing your logic. If you are unable to give me your word, how will I be able to trust you?

Mr. Spock: You see, Captain. Many centuries ago, the planet Vulcan was run by ruthless and dishonest men and women. They appeared to be honest. When they ran for office, they made promises and would say "I give you my word."

One politician who became our leader of the planet made a promise to the people. He said "If elected, I will cut taxes by half, and raise spending by half. Simply by doing this, we will balance our budget. I give you my word."

Captain Kirk: It sounds highly illogical.

Mr. Spock: Correct, Captain. Of course, the story does not end there. Our leader then convinced the Vulcans to wage war on the planet Romulus. The Romulans look very similar to Vulcans, and our leader said that the planet should be part of the Vulcan Empire. Of course, he just wanted their wealth and resources, and he said that the war would be very short, and we would be greeted by the Romulans as liberators. He said, "I give you my word."

Sure enough, the war lasted for years. Every year, our leader said that we would soon be victorious, and he told the people "I give you my word."

Captain Kirk: Certainly, the people would see through that after a while.

Mr. Spock: Unfortunately, they did not. In fact, people would mimic our leader and would say "I give you my word." It then turned out that because our leader gave his word, but never kept his word, he soon lost the ability to communicate. The Vulcan elders then saw that it was only the Vulcans who kept their word who were still able to communicate. The leader was then removed, and we made peace with the Romulans. We made it law and then custom that anyone who wanted to be in government must vow to keep his or her word. We found that when our leaders kept their word, our government ran much more efficiently, and Vulcans then soon embraced the concept of keeping our word. Because of this experience, giving our word is strictly forbidden. If we give someone our word, the sentence is death.

Captain Kirk: How logical.

Mr. Spock: Precisely, Captain. I can tell you that when I say I will be completely loyal to your command and to the Federation, you can be assured that I shall keep my word, as required for any Vulcan.

Mr. Spock was then hired. The Starship Enterprise then began to explore new worlds and go where no man or woman had ever gone before.

After reading these highly classified documents, I was reminded of another character I have written about in this book. Tommy Toughnuts always liked to look tough. However, when the going got tough, Tommy always got going. It did not mean that he would not give his word. His parents asked him to clean his room. He gave his parents his word that he would do so, but quickly left the house. When his parents asked Tommy to finish his homework, Tommy gave his word, and again left to go out with his friends.

Many years later, Tommy lost all ability to communicate. Yes, he could still speak, but he found that there was no one who would bother to listen to him. It turns out that if you only give your word, but never bother to keep it, after a while, there will not be anybody out there who will be interested in what you have to say.

It is this important lesson that will help all of us avoid Final Straw CrankaTsuris.

CHAPTER 37

SELF-HELP CRANKATSURIS

I HATE SELF-HELP BOOKS. Well, not exactly. I enjoy Chapter One of a self-help book. Chapter One typically introduces us to some common problem with that amazingly simple solution. It is like reading the last chapter of *The Wizard of Oz,* and the author is a self-proclaimed wizard. This Wizard then describes to us how he or she got to hand out the diploma to the Scarecrow, the ticking clock to the Tin Man, and the medal of bravery to the Lion. Now, start to read Chapter Two.

Let me take a step back into my history. I was married to a therapist for twenty years, and she was the one who ordered all those self-help books for me. I read each one because I was deeply in love, and always needed help anyway. She would quiz me on what chapter I was up to, and if I was only up to Chapter Five, there was disappointment because she had lined up four more self-help books waiting to be read. I always had to speed up to get to the next one.

Each of these books was typically written by another therapist. To be honest, it did not read exactly like *The Wizard of Oz*. Each of these books would describe the great idea that the therapist used with the therapist's patients, and I did enjoy Chapter One. It described a difficult relationship problem, and the therapist then described some thought process on how to improve communications and listening skills.

The rest of the book just goes on to bring up the same great idea with different patients, and the book begins to read like *The Therapist's Greatest Hits*. My experience then began to feel like I am sitting in the waiting room to get my own car fixed, and because I am waiting so long, the mechanic offers to let me watch him do another tune-up.

I say politely: "I already saw you perform four tune-ups, and I have no interest in entering the car mechanic profession."

Other self-help books have the one great idea, but at least, that therapist takes about five sessions to cure the patient. Every session has its own chapter. Of course, when Patient Number One is cured in Chapter Five, Patient Number Two walks in starting in Chapter Number Six.

All these books, written by therapists, were not the original self-help books. The original self-help books were illustrated children's stories. Wonderful illustrations, a fun story, great characters, and a heart-warming lesson at the end. It is the kind of story that you want to read to your child before they would go to bed.

However, these books had their own issues. The characters did not act in the way you would think they would act in the situation presented. Hansel and Gretel's parents decide to take the kids out to be eaten by wild animals. Can you really say that if you were Hansel or Gretel, your parents' decision to have you eaten alive in a dark forest would not upset you in the least? If you were Cinderella, would you really just take on that sort of abuse from three narcissistic stepsisters?

These two problems led me to write first a children's book *The Last Surviving Dinosaur: The TyrantoCrankaTsuris,* and then, the adult version, *A Grownup Guide to Effective Crankiness: The CrankaTsuris Method.* Both take on the concept of crankiness, but also, they are about knowing our true voice, and learning how to embrace it with both mindfulness and empathy.

Starting from the mindset of writing a children's book allowed me the freedom to start telling stories to adults. I wanted the stories to resonate with each reader. The stories present tools that the reader can use in their own life, and the story can be the anchor that reminds the reader of the tools that they already have.

Because each story talks about a different situation, and has a slightly different message, I stay away from being the mechanic inviting the impatient customer to watch another tune-up.

One of my favorite chapters in my *Grownup Guide to Effective Crankiness* book is titled "Drive Me Crazy CrankaTsuris." This chapter describes what happens when two sentences tied together start screaming in your head.

"It drives me crazy when…" and "I cannot understand how…."

This then sets up the story that follows, and we can see that those two sentences are pretty much universal for all of us. It is a common experience. Once we see that this is not just a personal affliction, we can then examine it, and start to be a little less crazy.

Now, I can give my advice to those people out there who also hate self-help books but may want to write their own.

The trick is to start by trying to write a good bedtime story. They are not just for the kids.

A Grownup Guide to Effective Crankiness: The CrankaTsuris Method

Praise for *A Grownup Guide to Effective Crankiness*

"I found myself laughing throughout every page of the book even though I was learning."   ~ Book-loving Tea Guzzler

"Hysterically funny and goes from dinosaurs to potato latkes to a pickled herring diet to flies, caterpillars, and worms."   ~ Diamond

Unlike other books, it deals with different aspects of Crankiness in an attractive way."   ~ NG

EPILOGUE

Looking back on this book, I shared many stories. But, one small story that sticks out in my mind is the story about the Rabbi asking about what we want to get in our life. The answer that he gave was pleasure. But, to everyone's surprise, the exact opposite, he explained, is comfort.

That, to me, is really what our Cranky Superpowers is all about. It is the celebrations we create after a whole bunch of crankiness. For me personally, nothing epitomizes this more than training for a half marathon or marathon, and then getting there, and then dealing with the difficult post-recovery sometimes. There is a lot of crankiness before you get to the finish line.

This past March, I ran the New York City Half Marathon. I have run the race before, and the NYC Marathon eighteen times so the running of the race wasn't the challenge. However, the story of the race itself really explains what Cranky Superpowers is all about. From the most experienced runner to the first time novice, there is a whole bunch of crankiness even before you start to run the race.

First, for everyone, there is the training. I get questions all the time. "Isn't it too cold to run?" "Isn't it too hot to run?" "Shouldn't you rest that injury?" "Why don't you just take a day off?" "Can't you just decide to sleep in?"

And, those are just the questions that my head and body are asking me.

On Race Day, I woke up 4:00 AM. The reason I woke up that early is because I needed to be in Brooklyn at the Wave Start at 5:45 AM. It was below freezing at 25 degrees Fahrenheit that morning, and with the wind chill, it felt like 15 degrees. Because I was unable to find anything else to wear, I wore my favorite sweatshirt that I did not want to throw away as my throw away shirt to keep me warm. I wore light gloves that did not really keep my hands from freezing because I never like the bulky gloves when I run. I drove from Hoboken to Lower Manhattan, parked my car, and headed to the subway. At that time in the morning, the trains run every half an hour so I had to wait on the platform for 25 minutes. Once the train arrived, I got on to the packed subway car. The subway car was even more packed than you may expect because that time in the morning, there is always an unbathed homeless person using up a whole row of seats on the subway car. With other runners pressed tightly against me, I took the half hour ride to Brooklyn.

After I got out of the subway, and walked three blocks, there was a 20-minute line through security to enter the Athlete Village. Then, there was the traditional half-an-hour line to get to the bathroom. It seemed like people spent extra time in the stinky Porto-Potty just to keep warm from the elements. We all had to pee really badly and everyone was doing the waiting to pee on line dance, jumping up and down, trying to stay warm.

All the runners then had to be in the Corral before 6:45 AM when the Corrals all closed. We were standing for another 15 minutes till we were able to begin to move towards the starting line.

Once the race starts, the runners had what I describe as the universal experience for all runners of any race. We crossed the Start Line, slowing shuffling in a packed crowd till everyone spreaded out. There were the hills you do not expect. There were the potholes that we needed to avoid. There were the traffic jams at the water stops. At every race, there is always the person who looks like they should be really slow but they pass you anyway. Then, there is the person who bumps into you because they have to run with earbuds listening to music, and they do not know who is next to them so they bump into you. On top of all that, there are always the Pace Running Groups racing past you to remind you that you can't run at that speedy pace.

But, on that frigid and windy day in March, after running across 42nd Street, when we made the right turn at Times Square, and headed up Broadway, all that stuff that can overload everyone with crankiness just disappeared. We were just a mile and half to the finish. We all felt that the celebration would soon begin. It became like a dance party in the streets. We were all superheroes showing off our Cranky Superpowers.

This is what I mean by Cranky Superpowers. This book is about what you can accomplish from a lot of crankiness. You develop your own unique Cranky Superpowers, whether it is running or anything else in life.

In *A Grownup Guide to Effective Crankiness,* I wrote about remembering how important it is to marvel. If you take time every day to marvel at something, chances are way better that you will have a marvelous day. If you spend time working on your own "personal" Cranky Superpowers, you may even get to marvel at yourself after you find your own personal journey to this wonderful celebration.

ABOUT THE AUTHOR

Steven Joseph is an attorney, seasoned negotiator, humorist, and avid marathon runner. He is a first generation American, and son of a Holocaust Survivor, which has impacted his writings that focus on our crankiness and overcoming obstacles in our path.

He is the author of a number of Award Winning Books including *A Grownup Guide to Effective Crankiness: The CrankaTsuris Method; The Last Surviving Dinosaur: The TyrantoCrankaTsuris; Snoodles, Kidoodles, Poodles, and Lots and Lots of Noodles;* and *Snoodles in Space: A Snoodle, the Zoodle Kidoodles, and One Happy Schmoodle.*

Steve lives in Hoboken, New Jersey, and strives to help the world manage their crankiness at his website www.StevenJosephAuthor.com.

Printed in the USA
CPSIA information can be obtained
at www.ICGtesting.com
JSHW081209111023
49714JS00005B/149